Poland
a tragedy

MICHAEL YARDLEY arrived in Poland with nowhere to stay and 300 dollars strapped to his ankles. For a month he toured the country with his cameras, an English visitor curious to see if the independent trade union Solidarity really was the greatest ideological threat Moscow had yet faced. He was the only western photographer trusted inside Polish factories during the general strike on 28 October 1981 and brought his film out of the country the same day. Six weeks later General Jaruzelski closed the country's borders to the West for the winter and declared a state of martial law. Michael Yardley is currently working with Solidarity organisations in the United Kingdom. This book is his personal record of a country waiting for doomsday.

ISBN 0 902129 38 4

ABY
POLSKA
BYŁA
POLSKĄ

POLAND
a tragedy

Michael Yardley

 Dorset Publishing Company, Knock-na-Cre,
Milborne Port, Sherborne, Dorset DT9 5HJ

International Standard Book Number ISBN 0 902129 38 4

Printed in Great Britain by Lonsdale Universal Printing Ltd., Larkhall,
Bath, Avon. Layout and presentation by Tony Pritchard and Colin
Graham. Typesetting by Margaret Oliver. Published by Dorset
Publishing Company at Knock-na-Cre, Milborne Port, Sherborne,
Dorset DT9 5HJ. Trade orders telephone Wincanton (0963) 32583

My thanks

I WOULD NEVER have completed this book had it not been for the constant help, patience and encouragement of my family and especially my girlfriend, Tara. I also owe a great debt to Professor David Martin of the Department of Sociology at the London School of Economics without whose help I would never have been able to go to Poland in the first place.

Rodney Legg and Colin Graham of the Dorset Publishing Company recognised the potential of my original idea and having done so helped forge a mass of illegible manuscript and a pile of photographs and posters into a book. This project is theirs as much as mine.

Bruce Page of the *New Statesman* and Paul Barker of *New Society* have given me the benefit of their long experience as editors and, no doubt sorely tempted on several occasions, have never thrown me out of their respective offices.

I would also like especially to thank Maria Jarosz, Maxine Pollack, Marek Garztecki, Janusz Bugajski, Krzysztof De Berg, Ludek Lasocki, Stefan Baran, Zbigniew Mieczkowski, Jan Chodakowski, Count Adam Zamoyski, Thomas Gatacre, Mary Sandys, Frank Spooner, Jane Thomas and Professor Ariel Lant MD, PhD, FRCP, as well as Ann Barr, Patrick O'Connor, and Robin, George and Sid of Chandos Photographic Services, London EC1.

The following organisations have provided material essential for the production of this book:

The Independent Trade Union Solidarity, Poland;

The Polish Institute and Sikorski Museum, 20 Princes Gate, London SW7;

The Polish Library, POSK, 238 King Street, Hammersmith, London W6;

The Solidarity Trade Union Working Group in the United Kingdom, 66 Philbeach Gardens, London SW5;

The British "Solidarity With Poland" Campaign, 9 Poland Street, London W1V 3DG. Telephone: 01-439-3658 or 01-437-1984;

The BBC Hulton Picture Library, 35 Marylebone High Street, London W1M 4AA;

Frank Spooner Pictures, London.

The Solidarity Trade Union Working Group in the United Kingdom and the British "Solidarity With Poland" Campaign are desperate for funds and would be grateful for any donations, large or small, sent to either of the above addresses. I would like to thank in advance any readers who feel able to contribute.

Finally, and perhaps most of all, I would like to thank the many people who helped me while I was in Poland. I hope that one day soon I will be able to return to their country.

In the beginning

I WENT TO Poland because I regarded the birth of Solidarity and its relationship with the Catholic Church as probably the most explosive event in European history since the Second World War. The outcome of the struggle between an independent trade union and a communist government would affect the whole world and, I decided, with nothing to prevent me, I would pack my bags and try to see for myself what was happening.

Cardinal Karol Wojtyla was elected two-hundred-and-sixty-third Pope of the Roman Catholic Church on the sixteenth of October 1978 after the death of John Paul I. As a mark of respect to the man who had died so suddenly Wojtyla adopted the name John Paul II. The election of a cardinal from a communist state was obviously going to have repercussions, especially as Karol Wojtyla was recognised not only as a scholar but as an astute politician as well; however, in October 1978, few could have predicted the birth of Solidarity. It would therefore be misleading to suggest the enthronement of John Paul II and his subsequent visit in 1979 to Poland were solely responsible for the creation of the independent trade union, but it cannot be denied that the immediate effect of this visit was to give the Polish people a new sense of optimism in the firm knowledge that they now had a true spokesman in international affairs. If a Pole could become Pope then perhaps Poland could become free.

During Karol Wojtyla's historic home-coming Poles turned out in millions to demonstrate spontaneously support for their Pope and the Catholic Church. Although it disapproved, the Polish state could only watch powerlessly as preparations outside their control went ahead and welcome celebrations were organised across the country. The experience and the sense of pride and self-reliance gained during these activities would prove crucial to the creation of Solidarity.

The Polish nation has one of the longest traditions of democratic government in Europe. When, after the Second World War, Europe was carved up among the superpowers, a new Poland emerged that had been reshaped and squeezed between Russia and East Germany. Poland's geo-political position has always been crucial: to the Soviets it is a buffer zone in front of their own western border.

Modern communist Poland has always had more contact with western Europe than her neighbours partly because it is a Catholic country that has strong links with Italy and partly because it has for centuries had close cultural ties with France and Germany. It also has a readily-accessible Baltic sea-port at Gdansk. But more important, perhaps, is the existence of a large emigré Polish community not just in western Europe but in America and elsewhere; it is reckoned, for instance, that there are ten million Poles living outside the country, with six million of them in the United States alone. Because these emigrants keep constantly in touch with their families and friends back home the Polish people are made very aware of current events and trends in other parts of the western world.

Poland suffered more than any other European country during the Second World War. Nearly a third of her people died, many in the gas-chambers of Auschwitz, and those who remained were adamant in their cry of "Nigdy Wiecej!" – "Never Again!"

But a new tyranny was rapidly imposed, that of Soviet communism, though even in

POWSTAŃCOM WARSZAWSKIM · CHWAŁA !

Official Solidarity poster that commemorates the Warsaw uprising of 1944 when, anticipating help from the advancing Soviet army, Poles rose against the Nazi invaders.

1945 the Central Committee in Moscow was sufficiently sensitive about the word "communist" to avoid its use in the title given to the official party in Poland. Thus, for almost forty years now, the Communist Party there has been known as PZPR which, translated literally, means "Polish United Workers' Party". In 1956, the same year the Hungarian people took to the streets of Budapest to fight off Russian tanks with antiquated small arms and Molotov cocktails, workers at Poznan in western Poland rose against their own oppressors and some were brutally murdered for it.

In 1940 the Russians had already done their best to cripple the country by massacring fifteen thousand of her officers in the woods at Katyn. This included intellectuals and professional men such as doctors, men who would have been vital to the rebuilding of the country after the war. They then tried to blame the killings on the Nazis. In the short term the murders at Katyn must have damaged any chance of Polish independence, but it was naive of the Soviets to believe that by liquidating a country's intelligentsia you could destroy its spirit. Dissidence can only be cured by freedom, not murder, and the day Moscow became the political capital of Poland a network of underground resistance organisations developed and spread. Their doctrine was not only resistance by guerrilla warfare but opposition by peaceful means too with a single objective: "Aby Polska Byla Polska" — "Let Poland Be Poland". These, however, were quickly mopped up by the Soviets and it is doubtful if any were still in existence after about 1950. Modern dissension dates from the student rebellion that broke out all over the country in 1968, as it did elsewhere in the campus world, and the various radical groups of both students and workers that were later formed in the seventies. Solidarity emerged as a direct descendant of these meetings.

In 1970, and for the next ten years, extensive dissatisfaction in the shipyards at Gdansk and amongst workers at Szczecin and in the Silesian coalfields in southern Poland led to the formation of a number of unofficial unions and dissident groups supported by intellectuals. These did not have particularly large memberships and, more importantly, they were not officially recognised either. Most influential of them was the radical Komitet Obrony Robotnikow (KOR for short), a prominent and vocal member of which was Jacek Kuron, a dynamic personality who later became an important advisor to Solidarity; ironically, Kuron was never a member of Solidarity because he was unemployed, and full-time employment was a stipulation of joining. Although it took its present form in the mid-seventies, KOR had already been in existence for several years. It was not a union but rather a group of sympathetic academics who gave advice and direct support to those workers who were trying to organise themselves.

In the summer of 1980 widespread discontent at the Gdansk shipyards again erupted, leading to the now historic strike in August. The workers decided to form their own independent trade union and took the name from their underground news-sheet *Solidarnosc*. Lech Walesa, an out-of-work electrician, who had often been in prison for his political activities, became its leader and first full-time employee.

Solidarity was far more than just a dissident group; it was a genuine trade union created, as are all real unions, by its own members, and existed in direct opposition to the fake official union structure set up by the Party. Sensing the danger to their established order, the authorities at first tried to suppress the news of what was happening in Gdansk — but they failed. As it grew, Solidarity organised itself on a regional basis, unlike the European and American unions, for instance, which have always been solidly founded on the nature of employment. Further impetus for the growth of the new union was the dissatisfaction felt by many at the rapid sinking of their country's national economy. In fact,

Solidarity poster of the unveiling of the Gdansk shipyard memorial. The three steel crosses stand 40 metres high and each is hung with an anchor. They were built at the yard to commemorate the deaths of between 400 and 500 workers who were killed by the authorities during the riots of 1970, and were paid for by workers' subscription. Carvings around the base include one of a group carrying a Solidarity banner.

the rise of Solidarity was inversely paralleled by the fall towards financial chaos caused by the ineptitude and corruption of Poland's communist leaders.

A general climate of change in official Polish political institutions, which included a slight moderation of the views of the Communist Party that first became obvious in the policy arguments of their Ninth Annual Conference in July 1981, had been accelerated both by Karol Wojtyla's election as Pope and by the state of the country's economy.

But by then Solidarity was coming up to its first birthday as an official organisation. The Gdansk union had grown so large and so fast that the government had been forced to confer official recognition on its status and on 31 August 1980 Lech Walesa had signed an agreement with Mieczyslaw Jagielski who was the state's negotiator. This agreement then passed through the High Courts in Warsaw, where it was ratified, and Solidarity became a legal body. A couple of days later two similar agreements were signed at other towns in Poland, Szczecin and Jastrzebie, a mining centre near Katowice, which gave official recognition to people in these areas who had also organised themselves outside the state-controlled workers' associations. These various unions merged under the single banner of Solidarity where they became a sturdy geographical skeleton for what was now a national organisation.

It was just ten years since, in December 1970, riot police and soldiers had gunned down demonstrating workers in the shipyards of Gdansk and by a bitter irony typical of East European bureaucracy a postage stamp commemorating the 1970 incident appeared in post offices across Poland on 16th December, 1981, just three days after General Jaruzelski's declaration of martial law. Its caption read: "To December's Dead".

Initially, under Walesa's charismatic leadership, Solidarity was apparently tolerated by the government — just. For a year the union thrived and pressmen from all over the world flocked to Warsaw and Gdansk. Governments in capitalist countries used its emergence for their own political ends and the fact that Solidarity was in many ways a very normal, socialist, trade union was lost.

It soon became clear that the growth of political, and especially industrial, unrest was not altogether to the advantage of the western alliance. Industrial problems affected Poland's ability to repay her crippling debt to European and American banks and financiers must have regarded the rogue union with some dismay because, for them, what better combination could there be than a well-disciplined "communist" workforce within a capitalist economy; their analysts only ever consider people as producers of profit. West German bankers, in particular, had made substantial loans to Poland, greedily over-extending their resources, and are currently in imminent danger of bankruptcy because of this. The finance houses who had irresponsibly lent enormous sums to corrupt Polish governments began to demand repayment with a louder and more united voice.

The economic pressure put on Poland by the West must be seen as partially responsible for the declaration of martial law, but even General Jaruzelski knew he could never regain the confidence of the international banks without the co-operation of the country's workers. The main reason for Jaruzelski's takeover was, without doubt, the threat of direct Soviet intervention, for the example that Poland was setting to Russia's other satellites was extremely frightening to the Central Committee in Moscow. Dubcek and his colleagues in Czechoslovakia had tried to liberalise their country in 1968 and the swift result was the appearance of Russian tanks in Prague.

But the situation in Poland was clearly different. Although many academics are members of Solidarity, the trade union is not a group of intellectuals. Instead, it relies for its strength on the working class and the

10

Solidarity poster to commemorate dates of significance to the Polish working class since the Second World War. "1956" is a reminder of the workers gunned down "by the forces of order" in Poznan in western Poland; there were disturbances across the country at the time and fears of Soviet intervention. "1968" is a reminder of the university riots and invasion of Czechoslovakia; "1970" refers to the Gdansk shipyard massacre, and "1976" is for the strikes at Radom and Ursus when KOR (The Workers Defence Committee) was formed by intellectuals to help the working class — and was funded by both groups; "1980" commemorates the birth of Solidarity, and a stylised Polish eagle appears on the right. The monument is at Poznan.

Russians knew that if they were to destroy the spirit of independence intrinsic to Solidarity they would have to openly rise against that entire workforce and be savaged for it by world opinion. In addition, the communist hierarchy in Moscow seems to have become extremely sensitive to international criticism since its disastrous invasion of Afghanistan. It is therefore not surprising that the Soviets quickly decided that the problem of Solidarity could best be solved from within Poland itself.

Leonid Brezhnev had tried a number of men before he finally settled for Wojciech Jaruzelski. He had been one of the million and a half Poles deported to Russia during the Second World War and had spent his formative years in an orphanage there. He was marked out as being potentially useful and, later, attended political indoctrination courses. Eventually, he could be safely returned to Poland as a "political officer" (as Brezhnev himself had been) in the certain knowledge that his first loyalty would always be to The Party; promotion in both the Soviet and Polish armies is based on this quality as well as an expertise in military tactical matters, two attributes Jaruzelski was soon to prove he possessed in abundance.

He quickly rose through the higher ranks of the Polish army and was in command of the Polish contingent sent in to crush the Czechoslovak uprising in 1968. He became minister of defence, an office which, in 1982, he has now held for fourteen years, and he was also an active member of some of the most corrupt governments in Polish history, though, until 1981, he had always cunningly managed to stay in the background of the country's political scene. Very little was known about Jaruzelski and this made it possible to create an image around the man to suit requirements; thus, he was packaged as a moderate and a patriot.

In October 1981, while I was in Warsaw, he became leader of the Party as well as premier, the only communist leader other than Brezhnev to hold both offices simultaneously. He was also minister of defence. The events that have occurred since then were not only carefully planned, they were inevitable. The only unanswered question is, when did the actual planning begin. It seems likely that Solidarity's growing pains were predicted and monitored in Moscow well before they became apparent at the union's First Annual Conference at Gdansk in September 1981. The Soviets, believing they had found cracks in the unity, decided it was time to act. Bureaucracy is always slow to set in motion, particularly when it is the bureaucracy of repression. Careful plans must be made and all contingencies considered. Once the blueprint stage has been passed, and in Poland's case this probably occurred in late September or early October, a couple of months are necessary before the physical preparations have been made and then all that remains is the waiting for the right moment.

The first warning sign must have been the enormously expensive Warsaw Pact manoeuvres around Poland's borders in September 1981 which coincided, intentionally or otherwise, with Solidarity's First Annual Conference. In planning his takeover, Jaruzelski's major problem was that he had very few troops on whom he could depend; most of the Polish army is conscripted from the general population who are largely sympathetic to Solidarity.

The blueprint was tested at the cadet firemen's strike in Warsaw on 3 December when army helicopters in conjunction with armoured cars and ZOMO riot police were used in a pattern that was later repeated in many other Polish cities when Jaruzelski declared martial law. Tanks or armoured cars would smash down gates or barricades and then a charge by ZOMO snatch squads and reliable soldiers would be combined with a helicopter assault. Once resistance

Lech Walesa at Solidarity's First Annual Conference held at Gdansk in September 1981. This is an official union picture given by Solidarity in Warsaw to Michael Yardley as a parting gift.

had been crushed less reliable conscript troops could be sent in as guards, their mere presence with rifles being sufficient to intimidate the civilian population who were unable to distinguish between one soldier and another. The same helicopters would then transport soldiers and ZOMO personnel to the next trouble spot; with so few reliable troops, mobility became the crucial strategic factor.

In the first days of the declaration of martial law, workers at Radom resisted initial attacks by the army and police by seizing weapons from the local arms factory — and then troops sent in to deal with them, probably conscripts, refused to open fire. Reinforcements were sent for and finally two thousand workers were arrested and interned in a camp of unheated tents outside the city in below-freezing conditions.

Jaruzelski's first move was to order the mass arrest of Solidarity activists from the leaders in Warsaw down to, and including, the shop stewards in provincial towns. He also closed the union's regional offices. At first this was a bad blow for Solidarity for its organisers were all either interned or in hiding. Jacek Kuron and Janusz Onyszkiewicz, the union's press spokesmen, were initially interned near Gdansk but were later flown by helicopter to "special accommodation" at Bialoleka on the outskirts of Warsaw.

But gradually, since Jaruzelski's takeover, underground bulletins have begun to appear with the heading, "The Resistance Union Solidarity", which call for widespread passive opposition. They have nothing to gain by provoking violent confrontation with the regime — passive resistance in the factory is vastly more effective. As this resistance spreads, a new underground Solidarity is developing, and observers around the world watch with concern the outcome of the Polish crisis. The people of Poland will not easily forget the feel of freedom.

RIGHT — Solidarity's essential supply of paper just after three tons had been deliberately held up by the authorities at the East German frontier. Photographed at the Warsaw headquarters.

"The Car of the Year". Tank on a Warsaw street: Jan Sawka's prophetic poster won first prize in the Eighth International Poster Competition in Warsaw.

Proletariusze wszystkich krajów, łączcie się!

Trybuna Ludu

ORGAN KOMITETU CENTRALNEGO POLSKIEJ ZJEDNOCZONEJ PARTII ROBOTNICZEJ

Nr 245 (11563)   Rok wyd. XXXIII   WARSZAWA, poniedziałek 19 października 1981 r.   Nakład: 975 200 egz.   Cena 2 zł   AA

IV Plenum KC PZPR

Tow. Wojciech Jaruzelski I sekretarzem KC

APEL KC PZPR
do ludzi pracy miast i wsi

Drugi dzień obrad

UCHWAŁY

— o powołaniu zespołu do przygotowania syntezy dziejów polskiego ruchu robotniczego

— w sprawie powołania komisji do spraw opracowania perspektywicznego programu PZPR

— str. 2

GŁOSY W DYSKUSJI
— str. 3-5

UCHWAŁA

Przemówienie I sekretarza KC

DRODZY, SZANOWNI, TOWARZYSZE!

Rozmowy przedstawicieli rządu i „Solidarności"
Podpisanie wspólnych ustaleń

I Zgromadzenie Branżowych Związków Zawodowych

Wybór przewodniczącego i wiceprzewodniczących Ogólnopolskiej Komisji Współpracy BZZ ● Uchwały

Front page of the Warsaw Communist daily newspaper the day after General Jaruzelski took over from Kania as leader of the Communist Party in Poland. It is dated 19 October.

RIGHT — Solidarity newspaper of 16 October 1981, three years to the day after the Pope was elected. The picture shows the board at the union conference at Gdansk and reads: "See you again next time".

Tygodnik

29 16 października 1981 roku Cena 9 zł

Program NSZZ „Solidarność" we wkładce

Diariusz zjazdowy: 5-7 października 1981 r.

Solidarność

I KRAJOWY ZJAZD DELEGATÓW

Szukanie właściwych dróg

Z „Olivii" nie docierają już odgłosy debat I Krajowy Zjazd Delegatów „Solidarności" będzie jednak towarzyszył nam przez następne dwa lata i dłużej. Dłużej, bo był to Zjazd pierwszy, a więc przez to ważniejszy niż te, co po nim nastąpią. Zjazd będzie towarzyszył wszystkim poprzez to co zrobił dla Związku i co zapowiedział dla kraju. Działaczom „Solidarności" dodatkowo poprzez zobowiązania, które na nich nałożył. Nam, którzy w Zjeździe uczestniczyliśmy jeszcze i poprzez sumę nowych przeżyć, obserwacji i doświadczeń.

Było to wielkie wydarzenie. Wielkie już choćby przez to, że po raz pierwszy od kilku dziesiątków lat obradowali w tej części świata przedstawiciele niezależnej i samorządnej reprezentacji ludzi pracy. Myślę, że nikt nie uzna tej oceny za przesadną, ale przecież byłoby niedobrze gdyby o randze Zjazdu świadczył tylko jego bezprecedensowy charakter. Nie po to powstaliśmy by odbyć unikalne spotkanie po roku, lecz by podjąć kwestie pracownicze, społeczne, narodowe — zaniedbywane, zapominane, celowo zepchnięte w zapomnienie. Powstaliśmy by sprowadzić kraj z dróg onych naszej tradycji i charakterowi, by odnaleźć drogi właściwe. I to jest odpowiednia miara dla „Solidarności" do której odnieść trzeba także Zjazd Oliwski.

Zjazd zrobił wiele dla tej sprawy. „Solidarność" rozpoczyna okres pozjazdowy mając wiedzę z normalnego wyboru, obdarzone mandatem zaufania przez reprezentantów 10-milionowej rzeszy pracowniczej. To są władze nasze, związkowe. Baczmy, by były zawsze blisko nas w kręgu naszych problemów i trosk, by działały skutecznie, by zachowały czyste ręce, by stroniły od złych metod. Zależy to wyłącznie od nas, od członków Związku, od tego czy potrafimy sprawować kontrolę nad naszą związkową władzą. To jest nasze prawo i nasz obowiązek i obowiązek strzeżenia demokracji w Związku. Jedynym bowiem panem „Solidarności" jest dziesięć milionów jej członków Ci, których wybieramy przeznaczeni są by służyć. Niech o tym pamiętają. Ale ze swej strony służmy im pomocą, zaangażowaniem, lojalnością i — nie waham się tego dodać — także dyscypliną związkową. Dyscyplina to znaczy uznaniem uprawnień tych, którym sami powierzyliśmy obowiązek kierowania Związkiem w obecnej kadencji i stosowaniem się do ich postanowień. Czeka nas trudny czas do przetrwania, wiele pracy do zrobienia ważne cele do zrealizowania. Sprosta temu tylko „Solidarność" rządzona i demokratycznie, i sprawnie.

„Solidarność" rozpoczyna okres pozjazdowy z uporządkowanym statutem, ta wewnętrzną konstytucją Związku, regulującą jego organizacje i zasady działania. Rozszerzony został zakres działania „Solidarności" uporządkowana struktura regionalna, sprecyzowane uprawnienia ogniw hierarchii związkowej, wreszcie określono kształt władz centralnych. Stało się to po bogatej debacie statutowej w I turze Zjazdu. Zadanie było bardzo trudne. „Solidarność" to organizacja ogromna, niezwykle zróżnicowana, pełna ścierających się interesów regionalnych, szczeblowych, branżowych, zawodowych, grupowych, personalnych, pełna różnych wyobrażeń o kształcie Związku. A jednak w tym kipiącym, pluralistycznym tyglu delegaci wypracowali uzgodnione rozwiązania. Spierając się, walcząc ze sobą, czasem wycofując podjęte decyzje. Dążenie do jedności, kompromisu i tolerancji przeważyło nad różnicami. Zjazd jako związkowa Konstytuanta dobrze wykonał zadanie. Mamy dopracowaną „Solidarnościową" konstytucję zbiór reguł postępowania, formalne podstawy demokracji w Związku Wszystkich nas obowiązuje jej przestrzeganie i jej postanowień, wszyscy musimy stać się strażnikami statutu związkowego przeciwdziałać jego naruszaniu. Jest to warunkiem naszych wewnątrzzwiązkowych wolności i naszego wpływu na to, co się w Związku dzieje.

＊

„Solidarność" rozpoczyna pozjazdowy okres ze sformułowaną myślą programową wypracowaną prawdziwie zbiorowym wysiłkiem delegatów, ujętą w po staci uchwały programowej a także zawartą w pozostałych uchwałach podjętych przez Zjazd. Dzięki tej wielkiej pracy Zjazdu wykonanej w obu jego turach i w przerwie między obradami plenarnymi — przez grupy robocze — wiemy dziś lepiej kim jesteśmy i dokąd dążymy. Wiemy, że „Solidarność" to związek zawodowy, obrońca świata pracy ale i wielki ruch społeczny, główna siła sprawcza narodowego odrodzenia.

Nasza racja bytu i wielka szansa dla kraju wiąże się z umiejętnym łączeniem obu tych ról, tak aby żadnej nie zatracić Dlatego troska o byt człowieka pracy każdego, a szczególnie tych, którym najciężej splata się w Programie z wizją Samorządnej Rzeczypospolitej. Tylko tam bowiem gdzie obywatele decydują o ułożeniu spraw wewnątrz kraju, pracownicy mogą liczyć że ich interesy bytowe będą respektowane Dlatego Program Związku traktujemy jako całość, której da się rozbić, podzielić na „czysty" i „brudny" nurt, na to co ważne dla robotników a co rzekomo im obce. Niech n kt na to nie liczy.

Dokument programowy „Solidarności" jest kartą spraw do załatwienia i praw do wywalczenia Stawia on Związkowi poza celami perspektywicznymi także zadania bardzo pilne, związane z sytuacją bieżącą, z nadchodzącą zimą, która niepokoi społeczeństwo i z pogłębiającym się kryzysem który czyni nasze życie koszmarem. Te bieżące zadania muszą być podejmowane już Tutaj program trzeba bez zwłoki konkretyzować i przekształcać w działanie. W każdej komisji zakładowej, w każdym zarządzie regionu i wreszcie w centrali związkowej trzeba zrobić wszystko, by nasi członkowie, ludzie pracy, całe społeczeństwo, uzyskali poczucie bezpieczeństwa, świadomość, że przed wszelkimi zagrożeniami chroni ich potęga zespolonego działania dziesięciu milionów członków naszego Związku.

To jest właśnie tym największym, najbardziej dziś niecierpliwym oczekiwaniem, które społeczeństwo wiąże ze Zjazdem „Solidarności" Sprostanie mu wymaga wielkiego wysiłku, Związek nasz stać na ten wysiłek.

WALDEMAR KUCZYŃSKI

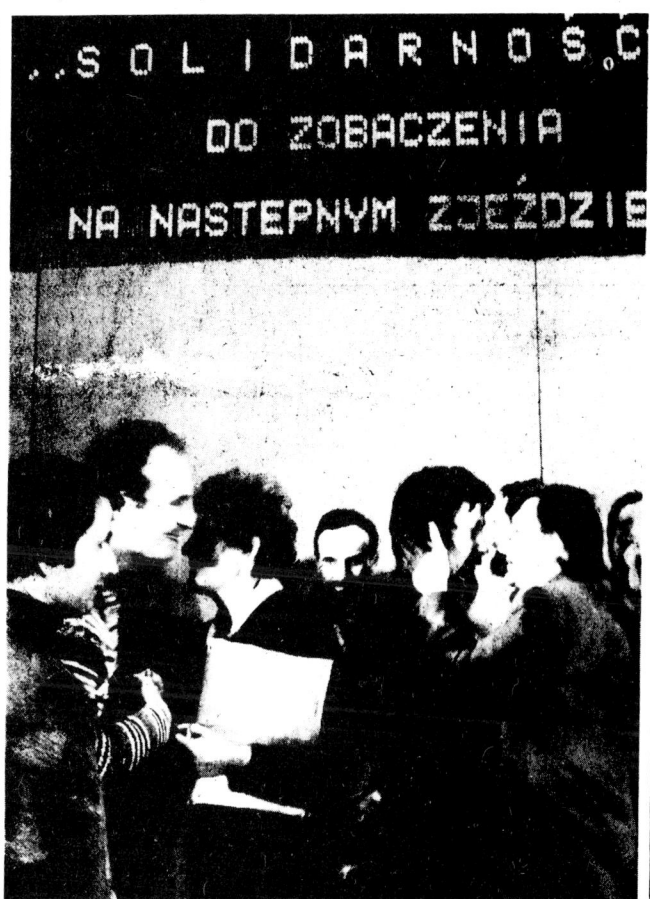

Fot. Lesław Wdowiński

Komisja Krajowa – po raz pierwszy

W długiej sali Rektoratu Uniwersytetu Gdańskiego z trudem mieści się cała Komisja Krajowa, czterech przedstawicieli Krajowej Komisji Rewizyjnej i paru dziennikarzy związkowych. Lech Wałęsa siada za stołem prezydialnym i krótko pyta: Kto jest chętny do Prezydium i wytrzyma ze mną pracować w Gdańsku? — n ech się sam zgłasza.

Podnoszą się ręce, wstaje po kolei Grzegorz Pałka Jan Waszk.. z Ja nusz Onyszkiewicz Andrzej Konarski Stanisław Wądowski Jacek Merkel Leszek Waliszewski, Wacław Adamczyk, Zbigniew Karwowski, Bogdan Lis, Grażyna Przybylska Wendt, Czesław K.. s. Elgunar Naszkowski, Patrycjusz Kosmowski Józef Patyna, Andrzej Piętpiechowski Ryszard Błaszczyk Stanisław Okoński, Mieczysław K. huta, Lech Dymarski, Anatol Konsik

Wałęsa sam dodaje do tej listy Antoniego Tokarczuka i Mirosława Krupi-skiego Mowi że trzeba jeszcze ustalić lu ludzi ma liczyć Prezydium składając się z dwu ekip stałej i dojeżdżającej Lech Wałęsa proponuje 19 osób na stałe plus 7 dojeżdżających.

J Onyszkiewicz przeciwia się, mówi że to jest w wiele za dużo i że z tej wł... i... się z czasem ściśle Prezy...

DOKOŃCZENIE NA STR.

BALTIC SEA

● SŁUF

● KOSZALIN

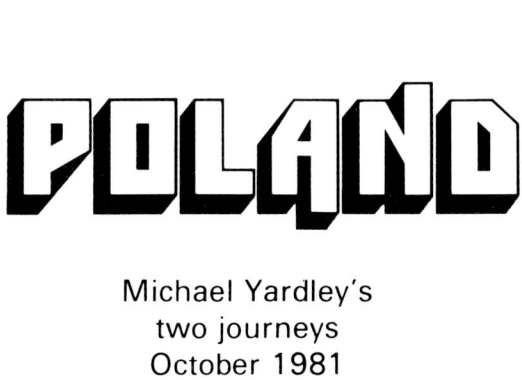

POLAND

Michael Yardley's
two journeys
October 1981

EAST GERMANY

SZCZECIN

● PILA

● GORZÓW
WIELKOPOLSKI

● POZNA

● ZIELONA GÓRA
●LESZNO

● LEGNICA
● WROC

●JELENIA GORA
●WAŁBRZYCH

CZECHOSLOVAKIA

0km   100km   200km

0ml   50mls   100mls

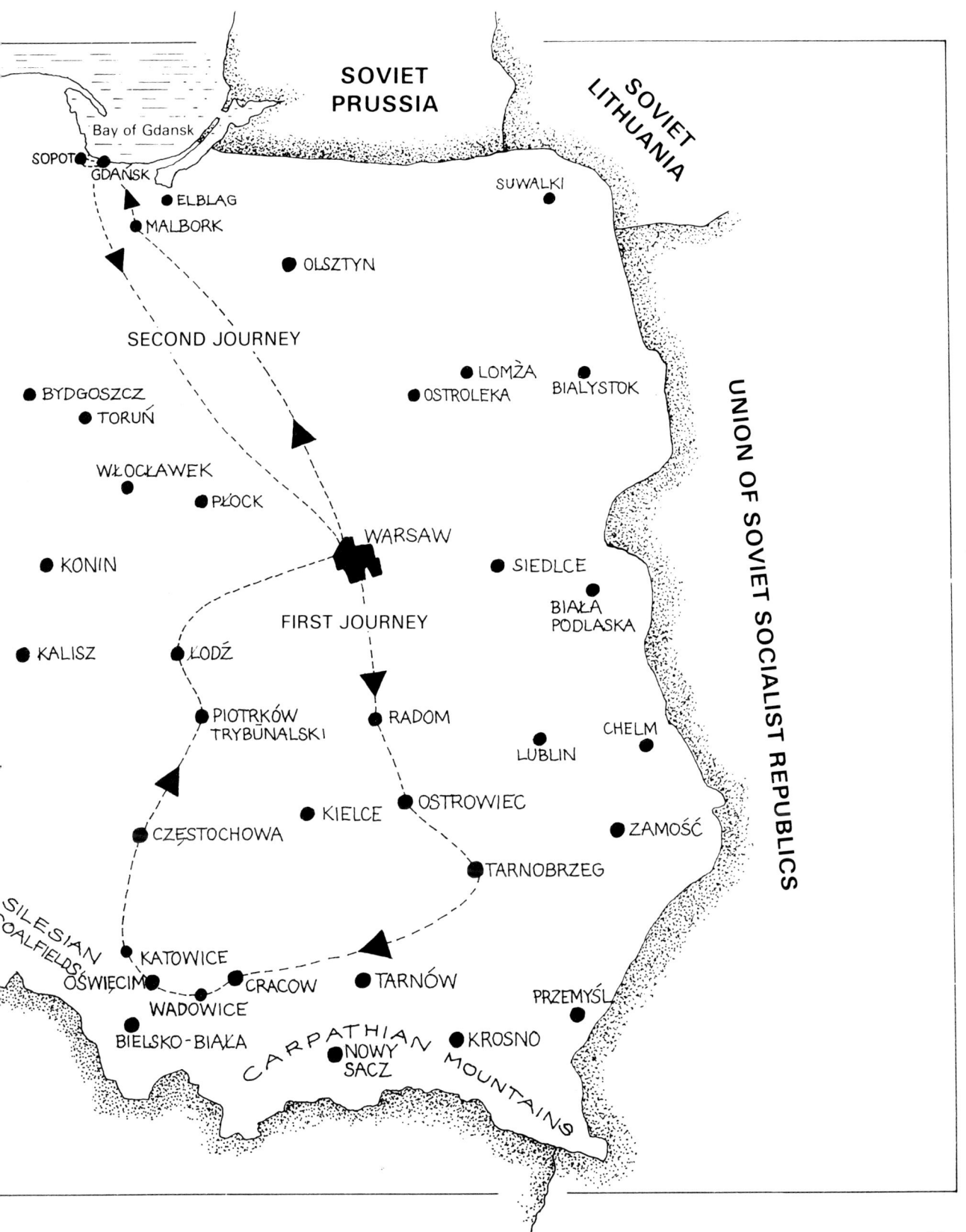

SOVIET
PRUSSIA

SOVIET
LITHUANIA

Bay of Gdansk

SOPOT
GDANSK
ELBLAG
MALBORK
OLSZTYN
SUWALKI

SECOND JOURNEY

BYDGOSZCZ
TORUŃ
WŁOCŁAWEK
PŁOCK
KONIN
KALISZ
ŁÓDŹ
PIOTRKÓW
TRYBUNALSKI
CZĘSTOCHOWA
KATOWICE
OŚWIĘCIM
WADOWICE
BIELSKO-BIAŁA
NOWY
SACZ

WARSAW

FIRST JOURNEY

RADOM

KIELCE
OSTROWIEC

CRACOW
TARNÓW

CARPATHIAN MOUNTAINS

KROSNO

LOMŻA
OSTROLEKA
BIALYSTOK

SIEDLCE
BIAŁA
PODLASKA

CHELM
LUBLIN

ZAMOŚĆ

TARNOBRZEG

PRZEMYŚL

SILESIAN
COALFIELDS

UNION OF SOVIET SOCIALIST REPUBLICS

21

October
1981

WHEN I ARRIVED in Warsaw at the beginning of October 1981 I had an overnight bag, three cameras, twenty rolls of film and one hundred and fifty dollars strapped to each ankle; on the advice of Polish friends in London I had also packed six bars of soap, a dozen jumbo packets of razor blades and a year's supply of toothpaste — the one thing I didn't have was anywhere to stay.

I took a taxi to the only hotel I knew by name, The Forum, and discovered that rooms started at fifty dollars a night when there were vacancies — which there weren't. The situation was the same at the other Orbis hotels; Orbis is the state-owned travel agency which runs all the major hotels in Poland.

It was a cold October night, but before depositing myself on some unsuspecting embassy official I had an idea. I'd been told by a fellow traveller that if I had any problems I should approach "students" who could easily be found at The Riviera, the hostel of Warsaw Polytechnic off Polna Street. So I hailed another taxi and asked the driver to take me there.

We drove about a mile down Marszalkowska Street, the heart of Warsaw's shopping district, and arrived at what looked like a large and rather characterless office block. I paid the driver and walked in. There was a large queue of people standing by the *Solidarnosc* (Solidarity) notice-board who were apparently waiting for the lift to take them to other floors of the building. I went over to them and asked, at first hesitantly and then more loudly, "Does anyone speak English?"

What seemed a very elderly student stepped out of the mass and to him I explained my predicament. He, as with nearly all the other Poles I subsequently met, was incredibly kind and did his utmost to help. Having explained he had no room himself, he then spent the next fifteen minutes making telephone calls and stop-

Students reading the latest news bulletins on the Solidarity notice-board at Warsaw Polytechnic.

ping people to ask if they knew anyone who could put me up. Finally, he said he thought he'd found someone and we took the lift to the ninth floor.

The gates opened and we walked along a grim corridor to a room at the end. He opened the door and a simultaneous burst of warm air and loud laughter broke into the cold passage. He said something in Polish to the occupants, briefly introduced me, and vanished − I never saw him again or had a chance to thank him.

I was in a small room with about six people. Somehow, four beds, several chairs, a table, a refrigerator and a wash basin had also been squeezed in − and this was nothing exceptional for throughout my stay it never ceased to amaze me how the Poles managed to cram vast quantities of people and things into small spaces.

Several of the inhabitants spoke excellent English and one of them, Stephan, told me I could make a bed up on the floor and stay as long as I needed. In the meantime I

was offered a cup of tea and a sandwich and Stephan explained that his room was not normally so full but he already had a couple of extra guests, one of whom was his girlfriend. Looking around, I noticed that someone had been travelling recently: on one wall hung an American flag with a Marlboro calendar nearby, and on another was a Mexican bullwhip. Beside the television set stood a large wooden carving of a Hindu god. There were travel brochures and American magazines all over the place, including a copy of *Playboy* proudly and prominently displayed on the table. A tape recorder, a bottle of Smirnoff vodka and a bust of Lenin stood on one of several shelves packed with English and American LPs and cassettes.

I spent the rest of that night bombarding my new friends with questions and trying to memorise their names − which I'm

Students crammed into one of the flats in The Riviera hostel in Warsaw watching television. Poland has just scored a goal against East Germany.

24

American Dream. Many Poles envy the freedom they believe the West can offer.

naturally bad at. They had all travelled outside Poland, principally to western Europe, but Stephan and his brother had even been to India and Asia as well.

After several hours of intense cross-questioning I found many of my illusions about Poland and the Poles had been shattered. I discovered, for instance, that these students knew my country and its history far better than I knew theirs. I had my first introduction to Polish attitudes on foreigners: "We like the Hungarians – they are our historic allies; we like the French and their culture, much of which we share. We also like the Americans."

"What about the English?" – "Oh, we like you but you let us down in 1939." I also discovered the Poles have very long memories.

I asked for their opinions on the growth of Solidarity, and was surprised to learn that although they saw the free trade union as a reliable source of information, they were realistically pessimistic about its chances of overcoming the problems of a bankrupt economy and high-level corruption.

Despite, or perhaps because of, my naivety, I was immediately accepted, a trust which I reciprocated and never regretted. I also quickly realised that Stephan was a man of some reputation which could only be enhanced by having an English guest on the premises – but I had no objection to being used so innocently. In all, I spent two weeks on the floor of that small room in The Riviera and I hope one day I will be able to repay the kindness that everyone there showed me.

Stephan, always the natural leader of the group, was twenty-four, balding, and a bit overweight. He was in his fourth year of higher education which would eventually lead to a master's degree in computer science; untypically, he was also a member of the Communist Party. He was not looking forward to graduating because, like

25

Women queue to buy stockings and other clothes at a shop on the corner of Nowy Swiat in Warsaw.

most young Poles who have the opportunity, he enjoyed being a student and wished to continue his studies as long as possible. Certainly, there were advantages in being a student: main meals were provided, there were special shops where the queues were shorter, and accommodation was very cheap. And through their own job agency students could earn more working part-time and during holidays than when they finally graduated and were employed in state-controlled jobs.

Particularly important for Stephan was the fact that students could travel abroad with minimal restrictions. He told me of ''business trips'' − which even extended as far as Dubai and Singapore − during which he would combine sightseeing with the purchase of consumer goods unobtainable in Poland to take back with him. Stephan was a natural entrepreneur; often, visitors would come to his room just to listen to his hi-fi (the best in the building), or to borrow his television or tape recorder. He was

always in demand, a popularity he shamelessly exploited when the need arose but in such a way that his innocent talent never made enemies, only more friends.

During that first week I slept on the floor at night, and by day Stephan, his brother, his cousin or a specially appointed friend, would spend several hours between lectures showing me Warsaw. Every night, in lieu of rent which had been refused, I would offer to take Stephan to dinner at a restaurant of his choice. Over the meal we would discuss my next day's itinerary as well as my more long-term plans. Stephan considered it his patriotic duty to be a conscientious guide and advisor so that when I returned home I could genuinely proclaim "I've seen Poland!"

The restaurants we visited had something in common with the Polish shops − no choice at all. After reading through a long and complicated menu at Shanghai,

ABOVE — Old ladies selling plastic carrier bags (some of which are overprinted "Duty Free Shop") for 200 zloty in a Warsaw subway. Such bags are essential equipment for the urban speculator.

BELOW — Two nuns wait to cross Marszalkowska Street in Warsaw to Our Saviour Church. Nuns are a common sight on the streets of Polish cities and they are frequently found queuing, along with everyone else, for food and groceries.

ABOVE — Bare walls, an empty cabinet and nothing on the counter. A shop in Gdansk. "Mieso" means meat, and "Wedliny" is Polish for pork-produce such as ham and sausages.

BELOW — More bare walls, rows of empty bottles and no cheese in the freezer. "Nabiat" means dairy. This shop is on a corner of Mokotowska Street in Warsaw.

ABOVE — The paradox of Poland. A street trader with old orange boxes for her counter and behind her a travel agency window advertising "Lot Qantas to Australia".

BELOW — On their way to work down Nowy Swiat in Warsaw, passers-by stop to watch street traders selling goldfish in jam-jars, and canaries.

Warsaw's sole Chinese restaurant, we were told that only wun-tun soup and chicken chow mein were available. I soon learnt that reading menus was futile and from then on merely asked "What do you have tonight?" Nevertheless, it was interesting, or rather disturbing, to note that if one had the money one could always buy a reasonable meal in a restaurant — if your conscience could reconcile you to the old ladies queuing for bread outside.

Every evening I would try and pick up the BBC on Stephan's radio. When, and if, I succeeded the room would suddenly fill with people anxious to hear the news. Although everyone watched the official Polish TV news broadcasts with interest, they were recognised as blatant propaganda.

My first days were spent wandering off down Marszalkowska and Nowy Swiat taking pictures and looking in the shops. I was intrigued by the little groups of pedestrians huddled together while they read the latest Solidarity bulletin pasted to a wall — and I was constantly shocked by the enormous queues outside many of the shops, especially those selling food.

The shops seemed very odd for whatever the facade outside depicted, the goods inside were always the same; books, clothes, toys, records, whatever it was, every store carried precisely the same lines. Around the corner from The Riviera was something called a "Pewex", the first I found of dozens all over Poland. In these one could buy West German and Japanese electrical goods but only with foreign currency. Even the prices were given in dollars. At other Pewex stores I visited I came across Levi and Wrangler jeans, Rose's lime juice, bars of chocolate, Canon and Olympus cameras, and most importantly (for the Poles) American and English alcohol. A pathetic sign at the Pewex in the lobby of The Forum announced both in

Place of plenty. Pewex, "the dollar shop", in Gdansk where Polish currency is not accepted. Its Warsaw equivalent proudly boasted: "We don't sell Polish vodka".

Polish and English: "We don't sell Polish vodka".

All the Pewex stores were doing a roaring trade, the very existence of these state-owned "dollar shops" helping to stimulate the black market where a dollar would fetch up to four hundred zloty when the official exchange rate was only thirty-three. Relatively, the pound and deutsch-mark, though in demand, never fetched as much as dollars on which all "black economy" deals were based. At these rates of exchange the average Pole making about ten thousand zloty a month could buy twenty-five dollars for a whole month's income.

Some people were making a fortune from the crisis and had a vested interest in its continuance. I witnessed endemic corruption in every public service with which I had contact; on railways, in hotels, in hospitals, everyone expected bribes. Poles who had travelled to the west might return with several thousand dollars, and the government encouraged people to open dollar accounts at the National Bank. Stephan, his brother and his father all had two accounts, one in zloty and one in dollars. Everything the government did promoted the formation of these two distinct economies, a bankrupt one based on the zloty and a second system based on the dollar.

The Riviera was only five minutes' walk from the Warsaw "Mazowsze" head-quarters of Solidarity; and after only a day in the city one could not fail but see the thousands of their posters and news bulletins which a team of men working through the night, at great risk, pasted everywhere as an alternative to the government-controlled press and television. Solidarity notices were read and discussed quite openly and the amount of apparent political freedom was surprising. A large

In addition to the queues, a common Warsaw sight was the group of citizens gathered around a Solidarity notice-board. Here they have been joined by a senior army officer, a colonel.

banner outside the Solidarity building read "Free Political Prisoners", and a badge I bought at the polytechnic had the English words "Russian Tanks — No Thanks".

As I watched the huge queues waiting for food or clothing I was struck by how comparatively well-off the students were. We simply cannot conceive of having to stand each day, perhaps all day, just to buy bread — and sometimes people would wait all night for "rare" commodities like meat. Whatever I write now, to understand the anger and desperation of the Polish people one must have actually experienced their ordeal; there is a tendency at the moment to say they asked for too much, too soon — too much bread?

I noticed many cripples in Warsaw and, later on, elsewhere in the rest of Poland. Frequently I saw an amputee with no artificial replacement, and it became apparent that there was a shortage of artificial limbs. I would find out later there was a lack of even the most basic drugs. And from the sheer numbers of people, especially young ones, who had lost an arm or leg, it appeared that Polish orthopaedic surgeons amputated more often than their foreign counterparts.

All over Warsaw there are little memorial plaques and shrines at spots where the Nazis executed hostages or committed other atrocities during the Second World War. No family in Warsaw was untouched by the occupation and I often saw old ladies praying or laying flowers at these places. It was Hitler's deliberate policy after the uprising to have Warsaw wiped completely off the map. In 1939 there were 300,000 Jews in Warsaw and now there are only

RIGHT — Most of Warsaw was destroyed by the Nazis during the Second World War and, afterwards, the Poles set about rebuilding much of the city as it had been. Horse-drawn cabs are still to be seen in the Old Town, and — BELOW RIGHT — there are places where an old man can pause for a cigarette.
BELOW — The Solidarity building in Mokotowska Street, Warsaw. The banner across the front reads: "Free Political Prisoners".

THIS PICTURE and — BELOW — A day at the races in Warsaw. The board has been cleared, the new list of runners has yet to go up, and the stands have temporarily emptied while everyone goes in search of something to drink. There is regular horse-racing in Warsaw and some of it is televised.

THIS PICTURE and — BELOW — More obvious drinking at Warsaw racetrack, and watching the horses coming down the home straight. Racing is popular in Warsaw, especially amongst the middle-aged. Both bar and restaurant are always full because they are usually well-stocked and drink is cheap. Often, when beer is difficult to obtain elsewhere, it can be found at the racetrack.

ten thousand in all Poland. After the war the Poles set about rebuilding their capital as a symbol of the general reconstruction of their nation and they made one proviso, that brick for brick, if possible, they would rebuild it exactly as it once had been. Old photographs and architects' drawings were searched out and gradually, over many years, an almost perfect replica of the old city was put together. The major construction work was finished by the late 1960s but it was only in 1978 that this mammoth task was finally completed. Like so many other things and places in the country, the Old Town came to represent the courage and tenacity of the Polish people and their ability to rise from the ashes of total destruction.

It was at the Palace in the Old Town, now used as a register office, that I watched couples being married and learnt that even if they preferred a church wedding they must still go through the state ceremony at a registry.

I visited the international hotels which were filled with businessmen and foreign correspondents, and I watched the telex machines being used non-stop. I saw the prostitutes in the hallways and the bars. As I walked into The Forum one afternoon the *milicja* (police) were in the process of arresting one miserable-looking woman for soliciting; foreigners are potentially an easy source of income.

The army's presence last October was becoming more and more apparent. On the streets joint army-police patrols became frequent, though usually the soldiers carried no weapons. Sometimes the patrol consisted only of young conscripted

The army's presence last October was becoming daily more apparent, particularly in Warsaw. BELOW — A parade in Victoria Street to mark National Army Day. ABOVE RIGHT — Constitutional Square where a lone soldier waits with a bundle of shopping. BELOW RIGHT — Each day country people come into the capital with flowers, fruit or vegetables to sell. This is a typical street market near Our Saviour Church.

A blackmarket "speculator" outside one of the markets in Warsaw has set up his open suitcase to sell shampoo. The price for one bottle in October 1981 was the equivalent of a week's wages. Other speculators specialised in soap or cigarettes.

town to sell their surplus produce. An orange box on the pavement seemed just as popular as an official market stall and all over Warsaw one saw hundreds of street traders. Outside markets there was nearly always a "speculator" selling shampoo, soap or cigarettes.

One evening Stephan's brother and his girlfriend took me to the cinema at the Palace of Culture. The main film was an English one about South Africa and apartheid, but before this we were shown a horribly graphic public information film about the consequences of not using contraceptives. There were pictures of unwanted babies who had been killed by their parents, in one case by hanging the child with a length of electric flex — horrible images I cannot forget which, doubtless, was their intention. The main film was dull but because of its subject, South Africa, the reactions of the audience were interesting. It was the first, but not the last, indication I had that the Poles are racially prejudiced. Although there are very few black people in Warsaw, there are a number of Arabs, especially Libyans, and these were detested by everyone I met. Stephan's brother said: "We don't like the way they treat our women."

I went into many churches and, apart from witnessing the obvious devotion of the Polish people, I couldn't help but notice that the Catholic church was running a parallel, but conflicting, anti-abortion campaign to the state's pro-contraception one. Again, there were the graphic pictures which I was later to see all over the country — a dustbin filled with aborted babies, a baby in the womb, a happy family, and so on. For what it was worth, this was the first objective sign I had come across that the church and state were in conflict.

The Palace of Culture and Science in the Name of Joseph Stalin was "given" by the

soldiers, who would strut along arrogantly to the taunts of other teenagers as yet undrafted. On television an enormous amount of air time was devoted to the army, its history and its "current role".

I visited the national army museum which, by now, I expected would be yet another memorial to the Second World War, but it was more than this for it tried to portray the Russians as Poland's historic allies. It was also the only museum where I was not allowed to take pictures which was a pity as it contained the most attractively presented displays of all the museums in Warsaw; elsewhere, generally interesting collections were often spoilt by bad presentation, as though it had all been put together by a committee.

Warsaw has many markets and every morning the peasants would come into

RIGHT — The Palace of Culture and Science in The Name of Joseph Stalin — the most impressive and most detested building in Warsaw. It is a permanent symbol of the Russian presence in Poland.

Russians to Poland. It was the most impressive building in Warsaw. It was also the most detested. Warsaw never forgave the Russian army for coming within a few miles of the occupied city in 1944 and then halting their advance. In anticipation of their arrival, however, the "Home Army" of partisans rose openly against the Nazis but after two months of bloody street fighting were eventually crushed and the Germans then took savage revenge. Poles will never forget what the Nazis did to them and understandably tend to blame all Germans for the murder and destruction of that war. But as more Polish people are now visiting West Germany, and like what they see there, it is towards East Germany with its Prussian associations that the blame is being shifted. Ironically, the Palace is no longer "in the name of Joseph Stalin": when the Soviet dictator officially fell from grace in the nineteen-fifties masons were sent up the front of the building to chip the dedication out of the stone facade – which,

rather limply, is how it now remains.

I had letters of introduction to the departments of psychology and sociology at Warsaw University but discovered that the woman I particularly wished to meet, a sociologist named Maria Jarosz, no longer worked there. Instead, she now had an office at the State Centre for Criminal Statistics.

Maria Jarosz was one of many astounding people I met in Poland. She had lost her job at the university under Gierek's government and been out of work for nearly two years. Eventually, she was offered a post outside the university at the Central Stat-

The German occupation of Warsaw during World War Two. ABOVE RIGHT – The Nazis have strung the bodies of executed Poles to an overhead balcony as a reminder of Hitler's single-minded determination to exterminate the race as a whole. BELOW RIGHT – A burnt-out German tank in one of the most fought-over quarters of Warsaw. The city was largely rebuilt in the three decades after the war. BELOW – Members of the Polish Home Army who rose against the Nazis whilst they were in occupation don the distinctive red-and-white armbands. Pictures from BBC Hulton Picture Library.

The ruins of Warsaw, 1939. The Germans laid siege to the city for three weeks a proceeded ruthlessly to destroy it with concentrated artillery and airforce attacks the centre. German troops marched in on 1 October 1939, by which time the num of dead and wounded among the civilian population alone amounted to about sixt thousand and of the buildings about twelve per cent had been totally destroyed. Nazi occupation was to last for five years. BELOW — German atrocities in Poland cartload of corpses. Pictures from the Sikorski Museum.

BELOW — A child of the Polish ghetto. From the moment they entered Warsaw the Germans began a systematic liquidation of the Jewish population. One of their first moves was to establish a "Jewish Residential District" which was cut off from the rest of the city by a specially-constructed high wall. But it was not until July 1942 that the Germans proceeded to "resettle the Jewish population in the East" and daily transports left the ghetto for the gas chambers in Treblinka. Photograph from the BBC Hulton Picture Library.

Warsaw citizens and the poster which appeared on the walls of the capital after its capture by the Germans during World War Two. It depicts a wounded Polish soldier showing a scene of desolation to the British Prime Minister, Chamberlain. The caption reads: "England! Thy work!" Picture from the Sikorski Museum.

Możemy natomiast posłużyć się innym wskaźnikiem określającym czy - i o ile - różni się nasilenie zachowań autodestrukcyjnych w poszczególnych grupach zawodu. Jest to współczynnik określający nasilenie śmierci spowodowanej samobójstwem w wyróżnionych kategoriach społeczno-zawodowych /w przeliczeniu na 100 zgonów danej kategorii/. Ten sposób podejścia do zagadnienia prezentuje tablica 4.

Samobójstwa według kategorii społeczno-zawodowych[a]

Tablica 4

Kategoria społeczno-zawodowa	Samobójstwa na 100 zgonów w danej kategorii	
	rok 1978	rok 1980
Ogółem	3,6	3,0
1. Kierownicy administracji, gospodarki, organizacji politycznych i społecznych	3,4	3,7
2. Specjaliści w zawodach technicznych	4,3	2,6
3. Specjaliści rolnictwa i leśnictwa	3,9	3,6
4. Specjaliś i w zawodach nietechnicz.	3,6	2,7
5. Pracownicy administracyjno-biurowi	3,9	2,5
6. Pracownicy transportu i łączności	8,4	6,1
7. Robotnicy w zawodach przemysłowych i górniczych	9,2	5,6
8. Robotnicy budowlani	8,5	8,1
9. Pracownicy handlu i usług	4,5	3,5
10. Robotnicy rolni i leśni	9,4	6,6
11. Rolnicy	1,3	1,3
12. Pracownicy o niewydzielonym zawodzie	6,3	4,7

a/ obejmuje osoby zawodowo czynne

Źródło: Obliczenia własne na podstawie danych GUS

Page from the paper prepared by Maria Jarosz that demonstrates that the suicide rate amongst the hard-core of Solidarity members has dropped since 1978.

istical Office where her activities could easily be monitored, and it was there that I found her. Most Polish academics know several European languages, as well as Russian, and we communicated in French.

Maria's special field was the use of statistical information on deviant behaviour (such as alcoholism, drug addiction and suicide) to predict the general health of society. Shown here is a page of her most recent paper which has been printed but not distributed. It demonstrates that from 1978 to 1980 the suicide rate amongst steel workers, ship-builders and miners, who make up the hard core of Solidarity, has dropped by almost half. She was convinced this was because these groups had finally found some outlet for their frustrations; frustrations which did not, or could not, of course, officially exist in a "workers' paradise". She predicted that as the government once more imposed restrictions the trend would reverse.

I arrived in Poland with just one word on my lips. Solidarity. Watching events from the West I had built up a number of expec-

tations, most of them wrong, about this independent trade union and it was hardly surprising that on my second day in Warsaw, having discovered the Solidarity building was only a few minutes walk from The Riviera, I decided to call there and see for myself.

Feeling a bit paranoid, and expecting secret policemen to jump out and grab me at any moment (the Polish equivalent of the Russian KGB, known as the UBEK s are widely feared), I walked to Mokotowska Street where I found to my surprise a large building crammed with people openly buying news-sheets and badges. Strung across the entrance was the large banner reading "Free Political Prisoners". I had simply just not expected this kind of freedom of speech and thought in an Iron Curtain country. It also struck me at once as impossible that Russian Marxism could co-exist with Solidarity.

On the ground floor at Mazowsze was a constantly updated permanent exhibition of photographs which documented recent political events, Solidarity rallies, and food shortages. All over the walls the latest bulletins and news-sheets would go up and were eagerly read. Many of the more important notices would be fly-posted throughout Warsaw during the night. At the entrance to the building was a kiosk where one could buy Solidarity badges and uncensored publications.

French, German and American press and TV crews constantly hovered around the place and upstairs was the "foreign section" where they went for briefing on the latest developments. The Mazowsze building was the second calling point in a three-ring circus for many of the Western correspondents. Most of the important foreign media representatives stayed in the

RIGHT — "Apel" — "Attention", to a list of four political activists imprisoned by the authorities. Notice-board in the Solidarity building, Warsaw. **BELOW** — The permanent, and constantly updated, exhibition of photographs in the entrance to the Solidarity headquarters in Warsaw with the notice-board and its group of interested spectators.

SOLIDARNOŚĆ
soviet tanks?
NO, thanks!
ABY POLSKA BYŁA POLSKĄ
I WALNE ZEBRANIE DELEGATÓW REGIONU MAZOWSZE
SOLIDARNOŚĆ
CZERWIEC 1981
ŻYWIĄ Y BRONIĄ
SOLIDARNOŚĆ
SOLIDARNOŚĆ
region MAZOWSZE
NZS

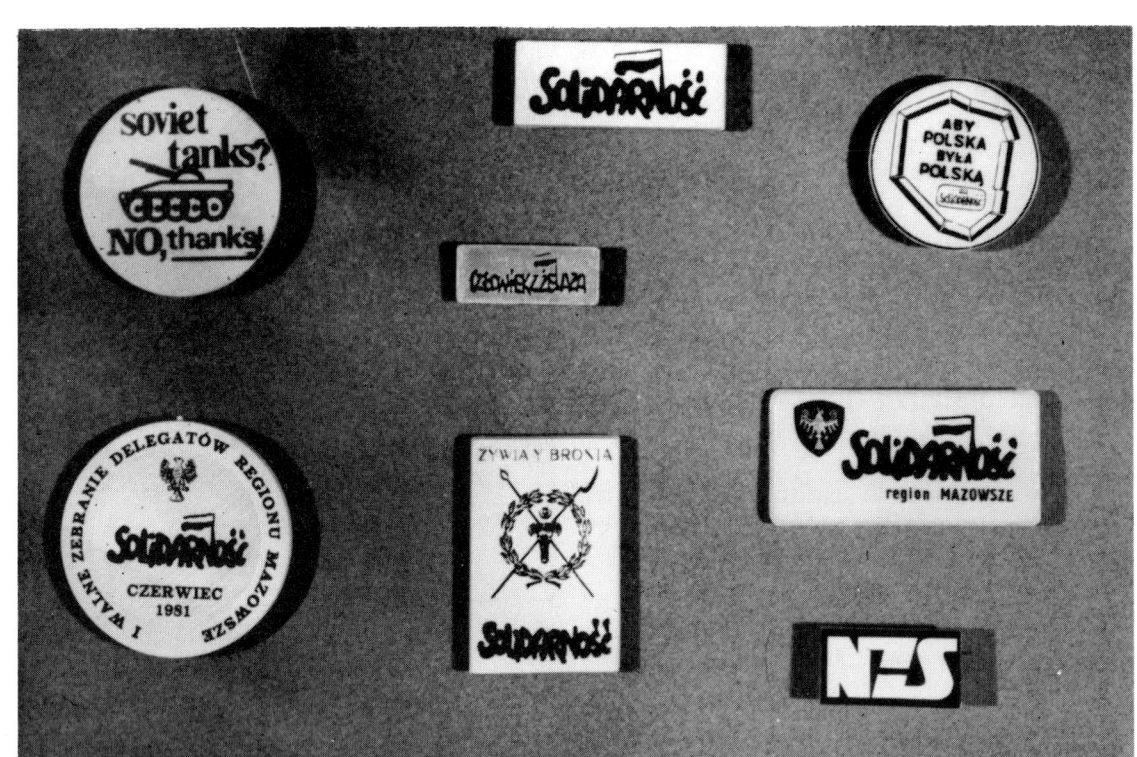

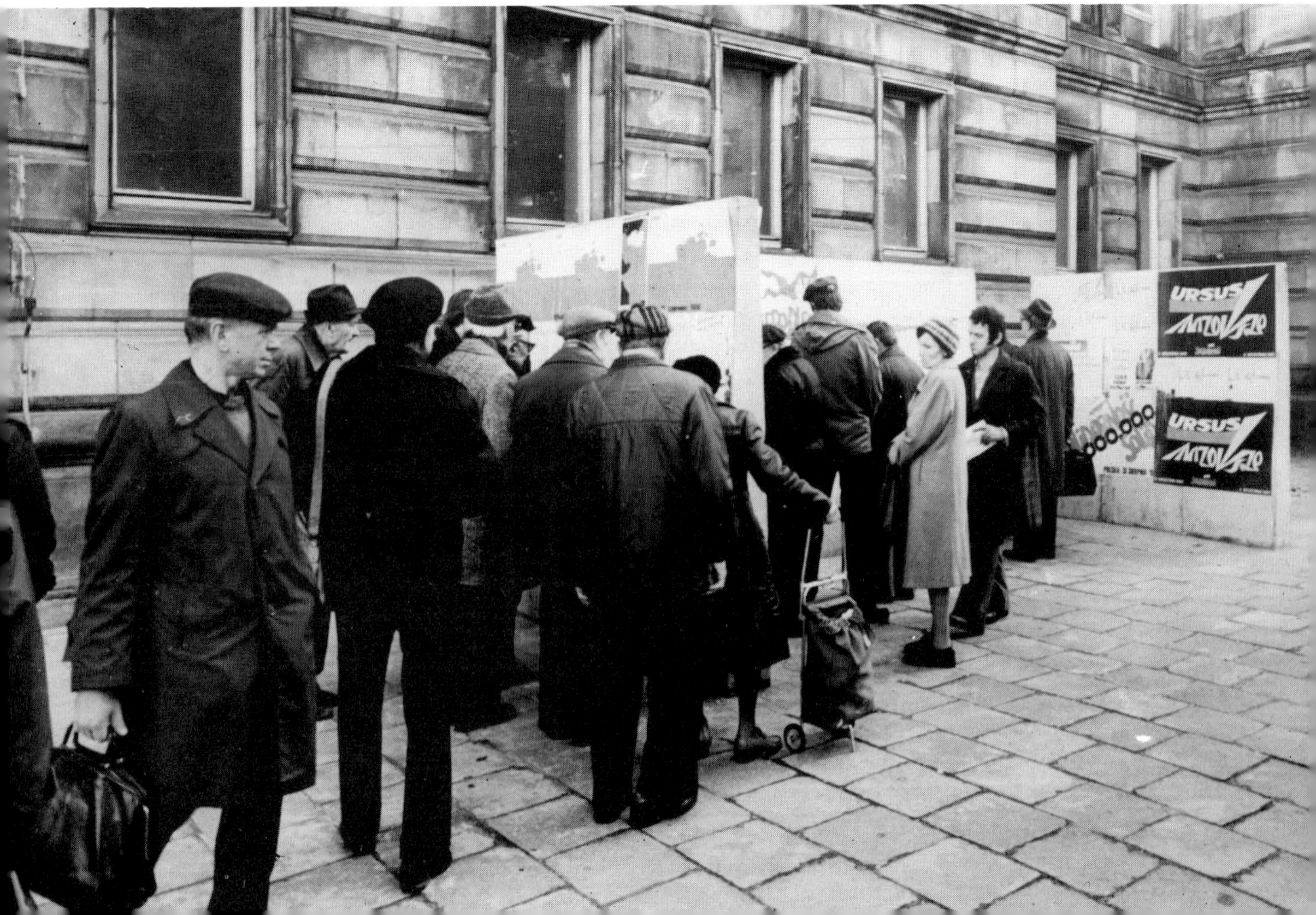
URSUS
MAZOWSZE
URSUS
MAZOWSZE

Victoria Intercontinental, the plushest hotel in Warsaw, and after breakfast each morning they would walk across Victory Square to the offices of Interpress, the official Polish news agency. From there they would take a taxi to the Solidarity building in Mokotowska Street for "the other side of the story" and then it was back, by taxi, to the Intercontinental and its telex service. The driver of the taxi, incidentally, provided the correspondents en route from one point to another with "what the man in the street is thinking". It soon became obvious that Poland, as represented by the Western press, meant just Warsaw and Gdansk, whatever the label. Again and again the reporters got things wrong because they could not be bothered to research their stories at first hand. To take one rather trivial example, a highly respected newspaper reported the badge "Russian Tanks — No Thanks" was on sale in the capital for three dollars when, in fact, mine only cost fifty zloty.

By a fortunate accident I met one of Solidarity's "foto-reporters" who invited me up to their office on the top floor of the building. Here, both photographers and graphic artists were at work and there was a silk screen press for producing posters, as well as a photographic darkroom. The first day I arrived the darkroom technicians were busy producing prints of an official Solidarity picture which showed Lech Walesa on his birthday; they gave me one which is reproduced here.

The photographers were using an odd mixture of Japanese, Russian and East

LEFT — Solidarity badges, including (bottom right) the NZS Student Union affiliation badge, above it the Mazowsze Region badge and (bottom left) the badge worn by Mazowsze Region delegates to the September 1981 conference at Gdansk. BOTTOM LEFT - Display of posters outside Solidarity's Warsaw headquarters. BELOW — The graphics workers who design the Solidarity posters seen at work in their top floor studio. The large poster reads "Independence" and, to the left of it, is a poster of the telegram calling for a general strike at twelve o'clock on 28 October 1981.

German equipment, and most of their camera bodies were wearing out through constant use; additionally, film and chemicals were in short supply. If there was anything useful I could do in Poland I knew it would be to help these brave and committed people and I volunteered to buy an electronic flashgun at one of the Pewex stores. This was a priority as many of their pictures were taken in poor light and there was insufficient flash equipment to go round. Their reaction to my gift was incredible: they offered to do all my film processing or, if I preferred, to use their darkroom myself. They also gave me ten rolls of precious black-and-white film which was currently unobtainable – a valuable gift as I had just run out of film.

It was a time of great activity and excitement. The first conference at Gdansk had been a success despite certain disagreements on policy, an inevitable hiccup in an organisation only twelve months old and built on rigid democratic principles, for in many ways Solidarity was a typical trade union. One had to be in full-time employment to qualify for membership, and students had their own affiliated union, the NZS. Its structure was strongly egalitarian which was not, however, typical of the general Polish attitude. At Mazowsze everyone worked frantically. They knew a government clampdown was imminent but could not predict when it would take place. I asked one journalist what she thought was going to happen: "I don't know but we'll go on working. How can you crush Solidarity? Solidarity is Poland."

Out of a population of thirty-five million people, nine and three-quarters were full members of Solidarity and over fourteen million were either full or affiliated members, as opposed to the mere three million

LEFT – Lech Walesa on his birthday, celebrated in September 1981 at the Gdansk conference. The first day Michael Yardley arrived at the Warsaw Solidarity headquarters the darkroom technicians were producing copies of this official picture and gave him one. BELOW – Solidarity's first annual conference at Gdansk in September 1981.

who belonged to the Communist Party.

After a week in Warsaw and the relative comforts of the polytechnic's hostel, albeit the floor of an already overcrowded room, I decided it was time to get out of the city and try to see Poland from a different perspective. Although constantly aware that I could never be anything but an outsider, I was still determined to see what the country was like away from its capital. Stephan had planned to drive to his parents' home that evening and asked if I would like to accompany him. I accepted, but they lived some two hundred kilometres south of Warsaw in Ostrowiec and we could only make the journey if we could get some petrol.

Stephan had an arrangement with a "friend" at a local petrol station who normally obliged him with a full tank after closing time in exchange for its normal cash price plus a packet of American cigarettes, and so, after lunch, he set off optimistically to see him. Stephan seemed to have a convenient "friend" everywhere but on this occasion the man was not at work and Stephan returned saying we would have to find "benzin" some other way.

I got into his car and we drove to several stations but while some were closed others had enormous queues hundreds of cars long. Stephan, who always boasted that he had never yet queued for anything and didn't intend to start now, suddenly stopped the car at a garage and walked off towards the pumps carrying a five-gallon can taken from the back seat. I stayed in the car rather piously contemplating the morality of his actions for he'd just explained that most petrol stations will sell fifty zloty's worth of fuel (about two litres) as an emergency ration to any stranded motorist who appears carrying a can — and you don't have to wait. He reappeared a few minutes later with his two litres and, after

People often queued all day for items that, in the West, are freely available. This queue in Warsaw, predominantly of women, is hoping to buy children's clothes.

some discussion, persuaded me to take on the role of the stranded motorist and go and get another fifty zloty's worth.

Stephan briefed me. "Don't say anything. Pretend you've got a cold. Just give the guy the fifty zloty and the can – he'll fill it." I was despatched feeling rather guilty and extremely nervous and found a pump surrounded by other can carriers. I waited a couple of minutes and, when my turn came, thrust both can and money at the attendant who took it automatically and put in another two litres. He handed it back and grunted menacingly but, fortunately, didn't say a word. Delighted by my success I returned to find Stephan rummaging around in the rear of his Fiat 500, the back seat of which was a treasure trove of survival equipment for contemporary Polish life. He re-emerged with an old hat and, with my borrowed scarf, he returned to the petrol station in his makeshift disguise and acquired two more litres. When he got back to the car, smiling, I

knew what he was about to suggest and, I must confess, I began to see it as something of a challenge. Equipped with spectacles and a Basque-style beret, I set off once more with the ever heavier petrol can. This time someone spoke to me but I grunted a guttural "Nie, rozumiem" – "I don't understand", and with a stubborn shrug of the shoulders picked up the can with yet another two litres.

Having decided that this was about as far as we could push our luck we set off to the next garage to try the same ploy. Not only was the can full within an hour but we had also found one particularly corrupt attendant who offered to fill it up again if we came back later and gave him a dollar. Which we did.

At about six o'clock that evening we set off for Stephan's home. It was my first experience of a Polish motorway and every now and again there was a crash and a jolt

A lane at Ostrowiec, some two hundred kilometres south of Warsaw. The cart is laden with sugar beet.

The crowded, polluted streets of western cities are a complete contrast to those in Poland where cars are few and, when they do appear, are all tediously the same. In this picture, taken round the corner from Warsaw Polytechnic, the young man on the left obviously dreams of other things. Two of the moving cars are taxi-cabs. INSET — Choice of cars available to the better-off Polish consumer: on the right are three Fiat 500s.

as the poor little Fiat hit a crack in the surface of the road. It was obvious that no maintenance was being carried out at all; in Warsaw I had seen one major flyover with large structural cracks in it, and many of the public buildings had permanently inoperative lifts. This part of the Polish landscape is very similar to Westphalia in Germany — very flat. Perfect for tank warfare.

Stephan's driving did not inspire me with confidence so I was thankful when, after about three hours of it and several near misses, we arrived at Ostrowiec. We passed through a very bleak town, far more typical of how I imagined an Iron Curtain country to look with its dozens of identical blocks of flats than anything I'd yet seen, and finally arrived at Stephan's home. Both his parents, I knew already, were Party members, and lived in a flat that went with his father's job. Their standard of living was not representative but, having said this, I should also point out that both were openly critical of the party they supported. Such criticism was quite fashionable in Poland during 1981.

We were shown into the living room where dinner awaited us, and it was immediately apparent that Stephan's mother had made a great effort to prepare a really special meal, a treat, in fact, that even Party members could rarely enjoy. Afterwards, I had my first introduction to real Polish vodka, that is "Rectified Spirit", not ninety per cent proof but ninety per cent pure alcohol. Claims are made all over the world for the local brew, but real Polish vodka leaves one quite speechless — literally.

A large Russian colour television set stood in the living room. It was flanked on both sides by cabinets filled with crystal, which is particularly admired — and made — in Poland. In one corner of the room was an East German exercise cycle and in another a rowing machine. Stephan's

Boy with a mud-sleigh at a small village near Ostrowiec. So many of the roads in rural Poland are without proper surfaces that the mud-sleigh is a common form of transport.

General food store in Ostrowiec, a very bleak town with dozens of identical blocks of flats.

father, like his son, tended to be overweight but the gym equipment, his mother explained, was mainly decorative.

There were stock-piles of neatly folded spare blankets and sheets in other parts of the room and, made to look as unobtrusive as possible, large cardboard boxes of shampoo and soap powder that Stephan had bought wholesale in West Germany; although his shopping trips sometimes took him to East Germany as well, his obvious preference was for the West when he could obtain a visa, and this in itself was doubly easy for someone like Stephan who was both a Party member and a student.

I was surprised not only by the quantity but the diversity of the goods packed into each room. There were more crates of soap and shampoo in the bathroom as well as boxes of razor blades and cans of aerosol shaving foam. One bedroom even had a spare refrigerator. The kitchen was packed to the ceiling with cans of food and I later saw the car had been moved from the garage permanently to allow more storage space. Here I found all the usual accessories of the do-it-yourself motorist — but in triplicate — as well as more food, batteries for torches, jerrycans and gas cylinders. Everywhere there were signs of preparation for the coming siege. Poles call such stock-piles ''speculation'' and thus black-marketeers become ''speculators''.

I had my first bath in ten days and slept in a real bed for a change. Stephan was very proud both of his home and his town and was anxious I should see all it had to offer. In particular, he wanted me to meet one of the teachers at his old high school and to visit the town's museum and castle. I was very curious to see a Polish secondary school and so next morning Stephan and I walked across the road to his old alma mater.

As with so many other things in Poland, the first things I noticed about the school and its pupils were not the differences but the similarities. These kids would not have seemed out of place in London. They wore jeans and T-shirts and generally looked and behaved like teenagers anywhere in western Europe. The building itself was quite ordinary, except for an exhibition in the entrance hall devoted to the army, the Nazi occupation, and Auschwitz. I later learnt that similar exhibits are to be found in every Polish school and that boys and girls must spend one hour a week on "military studies". The last war is a reality for all Poles, not just the generation that partially survived it.

Stephan went off in search of his old teacher and returned with a rotund middle-aged woman whom he obviously held in great awe. He introduced me as a post-

RIGHT — An old lady walks with curiosity towards the camera in Ostrowiec. BELOW — Queues again, this time for stockings at a draper's in Ostrowiec. Those with the foresight and cash, however, had stockpiled in advance such luxuries and were prepared for the hard times ahead.

graduate student at the London School of Economics working towards my doctorate – academics are held in high esteem throughout Poland – and the teacher crushed my hand and invited me in perfect English to be her guest in class that morning, an offer I couldn't refuse even had I wanted to. Much as he liked his teacher, Stephan begged to be excused and disappeared.

She was a very dominant lady, though not without a sense of humour. We went to the classroom where the students, all aged about seventeen, filed in and were then asked about their homework. At this point one of the teacher's eccentricities became apparent for it seemed she only gave written homework to the girls.

The class had been preparing to give dialogues on the subject of art appreciation. The two star pupils were called forward: "I like modern art. Do you like modern art?" – "Yes I do. An authority has told it is very good." – "Who was that?" – "A professor

of art." – "But do you like it just because a professor says it is good?" – "Of course not, but he knows more about it than I do and if he tells me it is very important I would be foolish not to like it."

Teacher smiled approvingly and a less talented pair were made to go through a similar routine. Afterwards, she rose from her chair and went over to the blackboard where she wrote: "I have visited every country in Europe except the USSR". She then asked various pupils to repeat the sentence until one small voice said from the back: "I've visited every civilised country in Europe with no exceptions". The class collapsed with laughter, the teacher looked embarrassed, and I suggested it was time I left.

Stephan had decided to wait after all and was sitting outside. We walked home for lunch. Afterwards he took me to the town

Autumn in rural Poland. An old lady fetches water from a well at her home in a small agricultural village near Ostrowiec. Collapsing buildings are typical of both urban and rural Poland.

museum, fifty per cent of which was again devoted to the army, the war and the Nazis. There were the by now familiar pictures of Nazi atrocities, evidence of local people who'd been in concentration camps or executed as hostages, and exhibits to show how Russian aid had helped after the war. There was also a Solidarity notice-board.

The town had been built entirely around a steel mill which poured pollution into the atmosphere at levels which would not be legal elsewhere in western Europe. We visited Stephan's cousins whose father had been an engineering teacher but now worked in the factory in an obviously less prestigious job — he was not a Party member. Although their flat was much smaller than the one where Stephan's parents lived, it too was stockpiled for

Alcoholism is a problem in Poland as elsewhere. In Ostrowiec the author watched young factory workers queuing for several hours to buy a bottle of bad beer. The picture — RIGHT — was taken at Warsaw Racetrack and the one — BELOW — in Marszalkowska Street in Warsaw. Drunks are a common sight in Poland despite the difficulty in obtaining alcohol.

doomsday. One of the cousins, a beautiful girl who loved music and played the guitar very well, couldn't afford records, let alone anything to play them on, but instead carried a notebook containing the lyrics of all her favourite songs carefully copied out.

I spent several days with Stephan's family and relatives and found this town very different from Warsaw. I watched young factory workers queuing for several hours to buy a bottle of bad beer which they then carried to a desolate patch of grass to drink.

I decided to take a provincial bus via Tarnobrzeg to Cracow where I would probably have to stay in a hotel as one of Stephan's friends there could not be contacted. I arrived in Cracow about two o'clock in the afternoon and spent the rest of the day wandering around but, for the first time since arriving in Poland, I was beginning to feel distinctly uneasy. Several people objected to my taking pictures. This had not happened before. Two Polish paratroopers acting as a police patrol noticed me snapping them and one of them started to run after me but, luckily, I managed to merge into a large crowd.

I saw another man, who was obviously a tourist, taking pictures in the Old Market Square with a new Leica so I went over to him, as I often did when I spotted travellers, and introduced myself. He was a Polish American named Jim, and a very friendly chap. He had flown from the United States to London and then on to West Germany, where he had collected a new, white, Mercedes convertible. This he had then driven through East Germany into Poland and had somehow managed to get through customs with a boot filled with camera equipment and film.

"The East Germans were only interested in whether I had a copy of *Playboy* or other pornography. They didn't care about the cameras." He'd then spent two weeks

Two Polish paratroopers acting as a police patrol in Florianska Street, Cracow. Seconds later one of them chased after the author who disappeared into a crowd.

BELOW — Main square of a small village en route between Ostrowiec and Cracow; the trees have all been planted since the Second World War, a memorial to the dead of which is on the right. Forty-two per cent of Poland's 35 million population live away from the towns in small communities such as this.

The church at a small village between Ostrowiec and Cracow in southern Poland. Two of the commonest forms of transport in the country are the Fiat 500 and the horse-and-cart. BELOW — Steam locomotives are still in regular use on the Polish railway system. This was photographed five miles from Ostrowiec and was pulling waggons from the steel-works there.

A vast queue waiting to buy shoes in Cracow alongside the voice of pop-dissidence: the circular road-sign (centre, right) has the word "PUNK" painted on it.

driving around Poland visiting his family and was surprised at the general reaction to his car — I wasn't: cars are even more of a status symbol there than they are in the West. A Volvo in Poland is on a par with a Rolls Royce in England, and as for a brand new, snow-white, Mercedes convertible, it and its inhabitant were like something from another planet.

Jim planned to drive across Czechoslovakia to Vienna and asked me what I thought of the idea. I immediately advised against it as I already knew the Czechs only permitted into the country one camera and ten rolls of film per tourist. To his credit, Jim still went ahead and telephoned a couple of months later to say that he had got through without any major problems. His story was an example of the divine protection of the innocent. If he had been less trusting and not totally sincere I'm sure he would never have got away with it.

Not unexpectedly, Jim was staying at the Holiday Inn at Cracow and suggested that if I couldn't find anywhere else to stay I should give it a try. So I booked a room by telephone and began looking forward to the experience of a Polish Holiday Inn. I could afford this extravagance because foreign visitors must cash fifteen dollars a day of vouchers which can only be spent in Orbis hotels and special shops — so far I'd spent none. I arranged to have dinner with Jim and a friend of his, a lady doctor, in the hotel's restaurant that evening, but first she offered to show us the cathedral and king's palace by night — both of which are quite magnificent examples of Poland's ancient heritage.

Later, and it was something of an anti-climax, we sat down to our meal. I'd just ordered a hamburger when a very tall man from the next table came over to us.

"Hi, there! My name's Dan. Here's my card. I'm fifty-three years old and married to this little Polish girl of twenty-five. Sure as hell make great wives, Poles. I'm in PR, that's public relations, and just so you know the kind of guy you're dealing with I'm in the hundred-thousand-a-year income bracket. Now that don't mean shit, but you know where you are now, upfront. I'm that kind of guy. I'm just a li'l ol' country boy really, ain't that right kids? (*turning to his table*) See those two boys over there? Well, I brought them with me to see if I can find one a wife. These Poles sure make great wives. No feminist crap and they work like hell. Hey boys! Come on over here and meet these nice people! By the way, do you know what a dollar's fetching on the black market? It was 380 yesterday.''

Recovery from the initial shock of Dan's machine-gun patter took several minutes and although I didn't find his personality particularly attractive I couldn't help but be intrigued by the man. He cross-examined Jim about his business activities but the latter, being somewhat introverted and very shy, made it clear he didn't want to talk so Dan turned his attention to me — and I was rather evasive.

He then insisted on telling us the rest of his life history. His wife's family still farmed in Poland and he'd come over to combine a holiday with bringing them a tractor: ''I really love those people — you wouldn't believe what I do for them''. If the opportunity arose, and he was working to ensure that it did, Dan intended to make a little money during his stay and he outlined several rather dubious schemes. He was leaving for Warsaw in the morning and, rather foolishly, I gave him my temporary address at the polytechnic; the truth is that I found his spiel rather fascinating and was keen to learn more of what he was up to.

For that one night I took maximum advantage of the luxuries offered by the Holiday Inn and used the opportunity to

A clothes shop in Cracow with its inevitable queue. Some of the onlookers seem to be wondering if it's all worth while.

stock up on lavatory paper, which was only to be found in expensive hotel rooms. I excused my behaviour by reminding myself that at fifty dollars for the night they wouldn't miss one roll. Since arriving in Poland I had not registered with the police as technically I should have done within forty-eight hours; if one stayed in an Orbis hotel, however, the obligation to register was waived automatically.

The next morning I accepted a lift from Jim who was going to Wadowice, the Pope's birthplace, and we drove en route through some of the most beautiful countryside I have ever seen. The Poles often refer to their "golden autumn", and no where was this more apparent than amongst the rolling hills just before Zakopania. We reached Wadowice and there I saw the church and the small house opposite where John Paul was born. There was a funeral procession at the entrance of the church and, having watched the mourners for several minutes, I then set off to spend an hour walking around the town. Food seemed more plentiful here and queues were noticeably shorter.

I decided to take the local bus to Oswiecim thirty kilometres away; we know Oswiecim better by the name given to it by the Nazis — Auschwitz. Having previously visited the concentration camp at Belsen in Germany I thought I knew what to expect, but I was quite wrong. There cannot be anything, I hope, like Auschwitz anywhere in the world. The entire factory of death has been preserved just as it was.

Auschwitz was started as a small experimental camp that was then methodically built up by its own prisoners until the name covered not one, but four camps in the same area. At its peak Auschwitz exterminated thousands of people a day. The place

ABOVE RIGHT — Spectacles taken from those executed at Auschwitz during the Second World War. BOTTOM RIGHT — Artificial limbs stripped from the corpses and — BELOW — the gates of the death camp at Auschwitz.

Auschwitz. Inside the electrified fence beside Watchtower D, with the death-sign in both German and Polish. RIGHT, INSET — In the ten months from October 1943 to the outbreak of the uprising in August 1944 the Nazis publicly executed in Warsaw over eight thousand men and women. After the uprising Himmler specifically ordered that every inhabitant of the city, every man, woman and child, should be killed, and on one day alone, 5 August 1944, possibly as many as ten thousand were shot by German troops. In the sixty-three days the revolt lasted about 150 thousand civilians died in Warsaw. Photograph from the BBC Hulton Picture Library.

HALT!
STÓJ!

has been preserved and, in some cases, rebuilt to give an idea of what living, or more exactly, existing, conditions were like. As I walked through the main gates with their wicked slogan "Arbeit macht frei" — "Work makes (you) free", I could feel a mixture of anger, nausea and fascination. I had some difficulty actually passing through the entrance because a group of German tourists thought it amusing to take holiday snaps of themselves standing by the sign warning of electrocution if one touched the wire. Some prisoners deliberately threw themselves on that wire to end the agony of waiting.

I walked from hut to hut staring mesmerised at the mechanics and relics of the devil — if any place on earth makes one sure of the existence of an absolute evil it is there. One room contains a pile of human hair and carpeting made from it, another has thousands of spectacles taken from prisoners, whilst in a third stands a stack of artificial limbs. There is a huge pile of suitcases and other items of luggage with addresses in Warsaw carefully painted on their sides as well as, on many, large white Stars of David. A mass of empty cans that once contained Cyclon B, the cyanide crystals used to gas the prisoners because bullets or hanging were uneconomic and slow, are a reminder of the many thousands killed in the factories of death. There is a cracked syringe used to pump phenol into the hearts of children when the Nazis were experimenting to find the most efficient way of completing their Final Solution. Hitler thought the Polish people as a whole should be eradicated with special attention being given to the "Jewish Problem"; in 1939 there were three hundred thousand Jews in Warsaw and now there are only ten thousand scattered throughout the whole of the country. Thirty per cent of Poland's population died in the war.

The Face of Auschwitz? The photograph is, in fact, of a painting at a gallery in Warsaw.

Auschwitz is not far from Katowice and this, I decided, should be my next stop. There had been grave reports in the newspaper and on television of unrest there and a Solidarity pamphleteer had been arrested by police, though a hostile crowd freed him and overturned the police van. I could afford, for once, to go by taxi though, in fact, with the unofficial exchange rates a taxi-driver would take you right across Poland if you mentioned the magic word "dollars" to him.

I had sensed a growing anger and desperation the further south through Poland I travelled, especially around Cracow, and although this had finally erupted at Katowice by the time I arrived there was no sign of any trouble at all. Had I known, I should have visited the factories and the mines out of town, but instead I went to the city centre which seemed quite ordinary except for the modernistic circular sports stadium and, everywhere, the enormous lines of old ladies waiting patiently for food or clothing. The queues here and in Cracow were longer than those I had seen in Warsaw.

I kept the taxi and asked the driver to take me around the place. Occasionaly he would park and I would go off on a short fifteen or twenty-minute walk but I soon realised there was little point in remaining in a town I knew nothing about and where I had no contacts so I asked him to take me on to Czestochowa. We passed a petrol queue that was over two miles long on the outskirts of Katowice and I wasn't sure if he would be able to get to Czestochowa even if he was prepared to take me. However, I need not have worried and when we finally arrived there, and I paid him off, he charged me just three dollars for a total journey of more than a hundred kilometres.

It had not been a complete waste of time visiting Katowice for it was there that I began to realise the shortages differed, perhaps predictably, from region to region. There were always queues for food but for other products there existed a popular belief that something unobtainable in one

Worshippers in Czestochowa, the spiritual capital of Poland. Nearly every Solidarity member is a Catholic.

town, such as razor blades or contraceptive condoms, would probably be found elsewhere. People therefore took mammoth, and often unsuccessful, journeys from one town or region to another on the already inadequate bus system, and the buses and trains were invariably overcrowded and packed with passengers far in excess of the official safety limits.

As the queuing grew worse, often lasting through the night, it was clear the increasing anger could not be contained much longer. I had gone to Poland because the synthesis of the Catholic Church and Solidarity seemed to me the most vital thing happening in the world and it was therefore natural that I should eventually make my way to the country's spiritual capital, Czestochowa — perhaps it was equally inevitable that I should find it disappointing.

I spent one night there at an Orbis hotel opposite Jasna Gora Abbey. My bedroom

Reflections of the church in Poland. THIS PICTURE — Jasna Gora ("white mountain") Abbey in Czestochowa, the country's spiritual centre, photographed on the hill leading up from the Poseidon Hotel where the author spent the night. BELOW — The courtyard at Jasna Gora Abbey. RIGHT — The queue for religious souvenirs at Jasna Gora. BOTTOM RIGHT — Worshippers in the cathedral at Cracow.

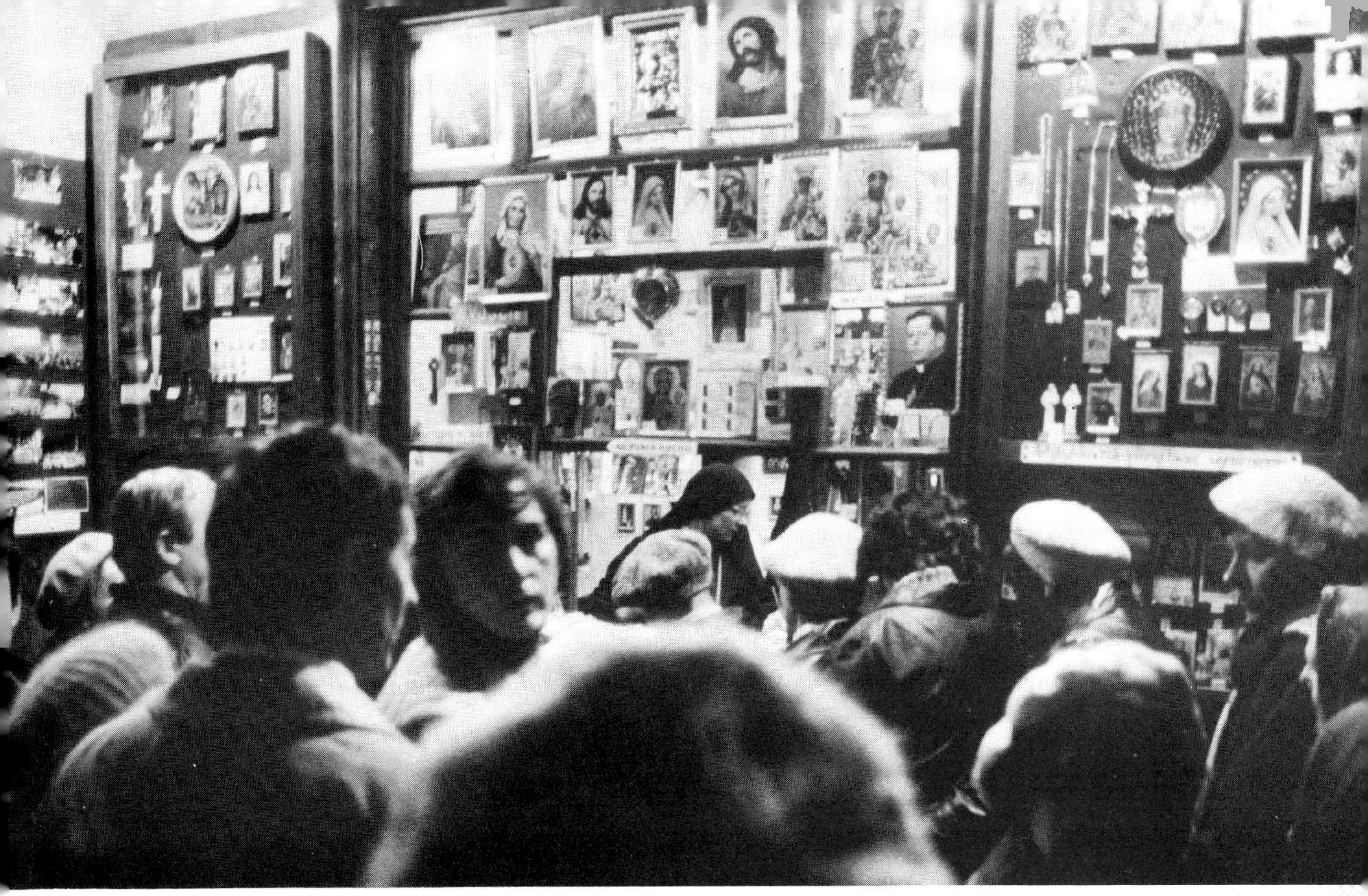

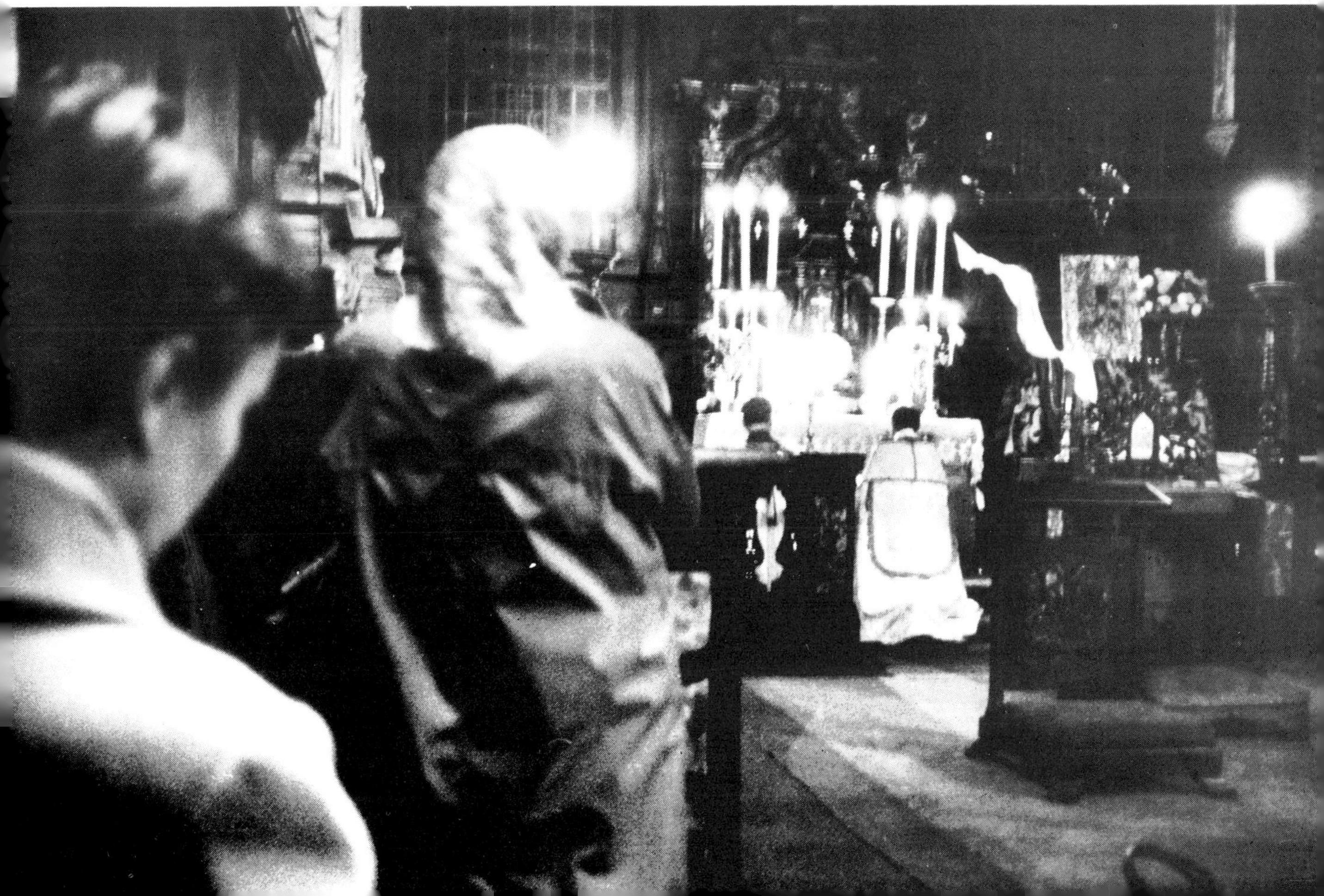

window overlooked the car pound of the *milicja* which was packed with military vehicles as well as the normal police vans; though sorely tempted, I decided it was too risky to try photographing them.

Next morning I set off for early mass up the steep hill to the abbey and was accosted by an elderly woman who insisted on pinning a cross to my coat and then demanding payment. I paid. The abbey is sacred because it houses the "black madonna", a replica of which is always seen on Lech Walesa's jacket. The first thing I saw when I arrived was yet another queue, though this time for religious trinkets at the abbey's shop. I'm a lapsed Catholic and I've seen the same thing at the Vatican but I was frankly revolted by the nuns selling plastic madonnas and other garish bric-a-brac. To me, this was not religion but mere idolatry and besides, the people buying the stuff were very poor. I raised my camera instinctively but soon found I was being chased round the courtyard by an irate nun. I hope her anger was inspired by guilt.

Later, I realised that although most members of Solidarity are Catholics there are very important ideological differences between the two organisations. The former's open governing councils are quite the reverse of the closed hierarchical structure of the church. It was a good thing that Solidarity and the church retained their separate identities for it enabled the latter to act as a mediator with the government. The government's attitude to the church had genuinely changed. Although the two had been in conflict for years, the Catholics with their innate order, were now looked upon by the Central Committee with something approaching awe.

It was time to leave Czestochowa and return to Warsaw. I decided to go via Lodz (pronounced "Woodge"), a medium-sized city east of the capital, so at six-thirty on a Wednesday morning I arrived at the bus station and found an impossibly large number of people all waiting for the same

Ladies waiting for a bus between Ostrowiec and Lodz. The public transport system in Poland is so over-crowded that fights for a seat are quite common.

bus, my bus. There comes a point in any mass of agitated human beings when a group psychosis sets in and everyone starts to panic. That point arrived and a fight broke out. Suddenly, it was as though we were no longer waiting for some provincial bus but the last plane out of Stalingrad. I heard a girl screaming and pushed my way through to find she had been crushed. Then the conductor grabbed us both by the scruff of the neck, hauled us both aboard, and the hydraulic doors hissed shut. Although there was hardly room to breathe, I managed to look around me at the people who, until a few moments ago, had been acting so irrationally. They were mostly middle-aged or elderly and were now quite calm. Some were even chuckling at their good fortune though, two minutes previously, it seemed they would quite happily have killed each other for a seat.

The bus was packed so tightly that

standing required no muscular effort though as I was jammed against the windscreen I was more concerned about protecting my cameras. These were always around my neck, but covered with a scarf and top-coat which could easily be opened; I'd become quite expert at whipping open the coat, taking a picture, and quickly returning the camera to its hiding place.

The bus stopped every fifteen minutes and gradually began emptying. Soon there was sufficient room for me to start taking photographs of the passengers but a man made a grab for the cameras and I stopped. The picture printed here was taken on that bus and, looking at it now, I remember the hopelessness in the passengers' faces.

I chatted to the driver with the help of my notebook and dictionary and, after about an hour and a half at the wheel, he started unwrapping his lunch — a piece of cheese in a hunk of bread — and without hesitation he broke it in half and gave one portion of it to me. The gesture touched me

but it was typical of the hospitality I found so often in Poland; it also contrasted with the other side of human nature I had seen earlier.

We arrived in Lodz and, as usual, I set off on foot to have a look at the place. I discovered that Pepsi-Cola was on sale; it is made under licence in Poland but is very difficult to find and although I'm quite fond of American soft drinks I knew my friends in Warsaw were absolutely addicted to them (like Western music, they are symbolic) so I bought several large bottles to take back. By now I habitually had a large carrier bag with me to take advantage of such finds.

I bought a ticket for the Warsaw train, which was on the point of leaving, and spent three hours standing in its corridor. I was relieved when we finally reached the capital. As usual, the central station was packed with soldiers but this time I noticed

Passengers on the bus from Czestochowa to Lodz.
Photography on the Polish public transport system is illegal and one of the passengers later made a grab for the camera.

several senior Russian officers waiting on the next platform. I went straight "home" to The Riviera, taking the tram up Marszalkowska and, for once, there was a seat; on all trams and buses in Poland young people are expected to stand if there are older passengers who seem to have greater need of the seats. I walked through Stephan's door at about eight o'clock that evening and found, not surprisingly, the room full of people watching television.

Probably the last thing I expected to find in Poland was a punk rocker so I was astounded to hear that a Yugoslavian New Wave group would shortly be giving a concert at The Riviera and that every punk in Warsaw would be there. For two nights the entrance lobby of the hostel was full of young men who, though not as outlandish as their British counterparts were unmistakably punk with their studded leather jackets and strange haircuts. At my instigation Stephan obtained tickets for the concert, but with some reluctance for

although he liked Western music he regarded all the punks as insane "narkomaniacs", that is drug addicts. Young Poles found Western music attractive partly because of its variety but also, and more importantly, because of its origin and the way of life and personal freedom this symbolised. Whether or not that freedom is genuine is irrelevant; young Poles craved it and in particular its manifestation as New Wave for with its characteristic alienation and frustration it seemed to represent in microcosm contemporary Polish life.

"The light's bad."

"Then smash it."

Thus replied Kamil when I tried to take his picture in the basement of The Riviera. Kamil was the ex-drummer of Kryzys, one of Poland's leading pop groups, and he

The punk revolution comes to Warsaw. RIGHT — Members of the "old school", that is pre-1980, in the basement of The Riviera. In the centre is Kamil and on the right is Kelner. BELOW — Punks in the lobby of The Riviera prior to the concert by the Yugoslavian band. BOTTOM LEFT — Polish punk at The Riviera.

spoke English with a cockney accent picked up from constant study of the Sex Pistols records.

"Are you the enemy?" he asked alarmingly, as I continued to photograph him. He'd started another group of his own in the basement of The Riviera which, incidentally, had been the birthplace of Kryzys and also Polish punk music in general. I went to one of Kamil's practice sessions which wasn't too successful as the group's lead guitar only had two strings and one of them had already broken and been clumsily tied back together; replacements could not even be found in a Pewex.

I talked to some of the other punks, many of whom spoke English. They fell into two distinct groups, those like Kamil and his friend Kelner who belonged to the old school, that is pre-1980, and the younger,

RIGHT — Robert "Afa" Brylewski, the lead singer, guitarist and composer for Kryzys, one of Poland's leading pop groups.
BELOW — Kelner and a friend attempt to repair one of the two remaining strings on the lead guitar; replacements could not even be found in a Pewex.

more recent converts who had adopted the music as open dissent became safer and more popular.

An older punk told me: "A few weeks ago I dyed my hair red and the *milicja* arrested me because they thought I was homosexual (*an offence in Poland*). Eventually they let me go thinking I was just crazy."

Nearly all the punks turned out to be students but this was not really surprising as the movement depended for its existence on word of mouth. The social pressures to conform were also much greater outside Warsaw. I was told Gdansk, too, had its devotees of New Wave for much news of the West entered the country here via the Scandinavian ferry routes. In the factory towns most of the working-class kids I saw had nothing to occupy them and just

LEFT — Lead guitarist and drummer with Szarlo Akrobata, the Yugoslavian New Wave band, who offended many Warsaw punks during their concert because "They're not real punks. They've conned us". BELOW — Group of punks wearing "Anarchy" badges pose in front of the Solidarity notice-board in the lobby of The Riviera.

wandered aimlessly around in small groups. They might have found the New Wave attractive – at least it's a cheap fashion to adopt – but it's doubtful if they'd ever even hear of it: the official media are rigidly controlled and the underground press is politically biased.

The concert was on a Saturday night and when I arrived, about half an hour late, I noticed many of the Warsaw punks were already leaving, evidently unimpressed by the Yugoslavians' performance.

"What happened?" I asked Kamil.

"They've conned us. They're not real punks." I later exchanged addresses with Kamil who glanced at the piece of paper I'd scribbled on and said: "Are you an upstart?" – "What ever makes you say that?" – "You live in London, S.W.7. Isn't that where upstarts live?" – "Who told you that?" – "I heard it on a record."

On the nineteenth of October the Warsaw newspapers announced that General Jaruzelski, already premier and minister of defence, had replaced Kania as head of the party and thus simultaneously held the three most important offices in the country. From that moment there was no doubt that the man who had been packaged as a moderate and a patriot was, in fact, a dictator. Jaruzelski was brought up in a Russian orphanage and, like all senior Polish officers, subsequently spent many years in the Soviet Union. To rise above the rank of colonel one has to spend several years at a Russian military academy, for promotion in the services and in government is based on one thing only, loyalty to the party which ultimately means loyalty to Moscow. Jaruzelski, who'd been minister of defence for fourteen years, now wanted to portray himself as a Polish Tito.

Reaction to his appointment as head of the party was immediate and hostile. A friend commented: "So we become more like Russia." Jaruzelski was now in a position where he could most efficiently crush resistance to his regime, and one didn't need a crystal ball to see a military takeover was the next logical step now that the three most powerful offices in Poland had been combined in one man.

This time I only stayed in Warsaw for a few days as I planned to spend a week in Gdansk and return via Torun and Poznan, which had been at the centre of the first major strikes twenty-five years previously back in 1956. I went to Mazowsze to process the film taken in the south and heard rumours of a general strike. I then looked up Dan, who was staying at the Victoria Intercontinental, and he invited me to dinner.

Dan met me in the lobby of the Victoria and was just as I remembered him – "Hey, I've got this great little idea". He introduced me to another American, an economist and a vice-president of a large American corporation, who frequently visited Warsaw because of the Polish government's enormous outstanding debt to his company. He had met Dan by chance and found himself as intrigued as I was by the man's "upfront" approach to everything. We all had dinner together and for the first time in my life I ate bison – it was the Victoria's speciality, but a bit tough. I found John, the economist, very alert to the changing situation in Poland. He predicted an imminent declaration of a "state of emergency" and made a very perceptive analysis of the country's economic ills. Basically, he believed these resulted from the inflexibility of the Communist regime's economic planning and the fact that it had backed heavy industry rather than high technology. He added that everyone was on the fiddle and believed the Russians would never come to the financial aid of the country. John told me how one Japanese company had given ten thousand dollar bribes to foreign trade officials when Poland had been "buying" before the general economic collapse; he added that he'd also attended the funeral of the Polish friend who'd given him that piece of information and who'd been found beaten to death in a public lavatory.

After an extremely involved conversation, Dan, who'd remain uncharacteristically silent throughout, brought us back to a different kind of reality with a bang. He astonished me with the news that one of his sons had found a Polish wife after all and that both boys and the new bride were considering going to Gdansk. As I'd already mentioned this was precisely what I intended doing the next day he asked if I'd mind "looking after" them, as he called it, because he was flying off to Madrid. They were both several years older than me, and foolishly I accepted.

John invited me back for lunch the next day along with a girl he knew from Interpress, and it was arranged that I should catch the four o'clock train, with the boys, afterwards. Until then I knew very little about Dan's two sons: they had always seemed dominated by the presence of their father and, by comparison, seemed fairly normal to the point of dullness.

Next morning I bought tickets for the journey, visited the Zacheta gallery, and walked to the Victoria, where I spent several hours with John and the girl from the news agency. It may have been a coincidence that an important American businessman had a girlfriend who worked for Interpress, but I doubt it. John was nobody's fool. He was always extremely relaxed and I saw in him the type of man accustomed to working in dangerous situations. He taught me a lot about Poland and, later, did several important favours for me from which he not only put himself at risk but could not have made any personal gain whatsoever. John also advised me against acting as babysitter for Dan's two boys, but I was already committed.

Whilst we were having lunch there was a commotion from another table where my future charges had just ordered four Chateaubriands and two bottles of champagne which it transpired they intended should serve as a sort of picnic meal for the journey. I sent a message across suggesting we should consider

leaving or we'd miss the train.

We met at the reception desk where I found the two young men in a considerable state of excitement but the new bride showing markedly less enthusiasm. I was even more perplexed when the non-married American told me his recently acquired sister-in-law had proved to be a virgin and what a delightful and unexpected bonus this had been for his brother. Eventually we managed to get a taxi and, after an argument between the happy couple, drove to the station.

The train was already waiting but before we could board it a stranger from the crowd tried to grab one of the boys' wallets. The two of them caught the culprit but the man broke free, dropped the contents of the wallet, and now the platform was covered in dollar bills. This was an unexpected pleasure for lots of people.

It's a long journey to Gdansk, or Danzig as it was called before the war, and as I didn't intend standing for five hours I had booked seats in advance. The Americans quickly settled down and immediately began to unpack their meal, much to the bewilderment of the other occupants of the compartment who were not expecting to see a bottle of champagne emerge from a suitcase. They were even more surprised to be offered a glass of it which was itself soon followed by offers of chewing gum and Chateaubriand sandwiches. Nearly everyone accepted something but I was rather embarrassed by this "beads for the natives" attitude and went to sleep.

When I awoke I discovered the boys had vanished so I took advantage of this momentary respite and struck up a conversation with a woman sitting opposite my window seat. It transpired she was a professor at Gdansk university and had been a Cambridge research fellow in the thirties so her English was naturally perfect. I told her the story of my American companions and their Polish wife which she found so amusing that she recounted it to everyone else in the compartment. This initiated a general heated discussion, in Polish of course, about love and marriage which I was unable to follow. I did gather, however, from one of the passengers that there was a typhoid epidemic in Gdansk which was rather disturbing news for I had, as yet, nowhere to stay when I arrived and I was also running very short of cash. I chatted on for a couple of hours and eventually went back to sleep again.

I awoke this time to find everyone staring out of the compartment door at something happening further down the corridor and had a horrible suspicion as to what, or who, it might be. I got up and went out to find an extremely fat English woman, who claimed to be a foreign correspondent, engaged in a heavy drinking bout with several Polish soldiers and my two Americans. The first thing she did was ask me if I were a member of the National Union of Journalists, which seemed a fairly irrelevant question under the circumstances, and she then stated flatly that if I wasn't she would not act as translator — which I hadn't asked her to do anyway. There was one other small problem: Dan's younger son was now wearing a Polish army uniform. This was a rather delicate situation for I noticed huddled in a corner a pathetic looking chap wearing just vest and underpants and sucking at a bottle of champagne. He was obviously the last owner of the American's new clothes and I suggested to them both that this was really not a very good idea.

They told me everything was all right, but I was not convinced. They had, they said, merely swapped a bottle of champagne for a bottle of vodka — and the results were apparent. To aggravate an already tense situation one of the boys produced a Kodak Instamatic with flash attachment and said he wanted a picture to show the folks back home. Again, I attempted to explain that this was rather a silly thing to do for not only had I begun to suspect that the drunken Polish soldiers were a bit camera shy I also knew it was a criminal offence to take photographs on the trans-

port system. But to no avail.

It was clear that the atmosphere of bon homie was now extremely fragile and after several further attempts to persuade them to return to their seats I decided the point was quickly arriving where duty ended and self-preservation began. The first flash-bulb popped and it was obviously time for me to leave. That this was a prudent decision was soon confirmed for I had just reached my seat when there was an enormous anguished cry from up the corridor followed by a series of thumps and crashes and the train began to slow down. When another group of soldiers rushed past the window of my compartment I thought it might be wise to grab my cameras and jump off; the authorities, I knew, would have taken a dim view of my collection of camera equipment and an even dimmer view of my film if they'd got around to processing it.

My sudden exit came as a bit of a surprise to the lady professor from Gdansk but, sadly, I didn't have time to explain. Just as the train slowed down to a safe speed I jumped — and found myself on the very edge of a platform. I had not had time to give careful consideration to my actions but I was now certain that my panic decision had been the right one for at that moment a group of people obviously involved in some kind of fracas spilled off the train and onto the station platform. I stood watching but, after several minutes, everyone calmed down, climbed back on board, and the train continued its journey.

My problem now was what to do next. According to a sign I was in a place called Malbork which is not more than about a hundred kilometres from Gdansk. "Approach students", I remembered. The first person I went up to spoke no English but the second understood me and said he was a student of architecture at Gdansk Polytechnic, a strange coincidence. I told him exactly what had happened and why I was travelling round Poland and he cheered me immensely by telling me not to

Excuse for a military presence on the streets of Warsaw: guarding the Tomb of the Unknown Soldier in Victory Square. BELOW — Opposite the tomb, on the other side of the square, is the headquarters of the army. Translated, the sign reads: "People's Army of Poland — Faithful Defender of Socialism and Polish Independence". The remaining sides of Victory Square contain the buildings of Interpress, the state news agency, and the Victoria Intercontinental Hotel.

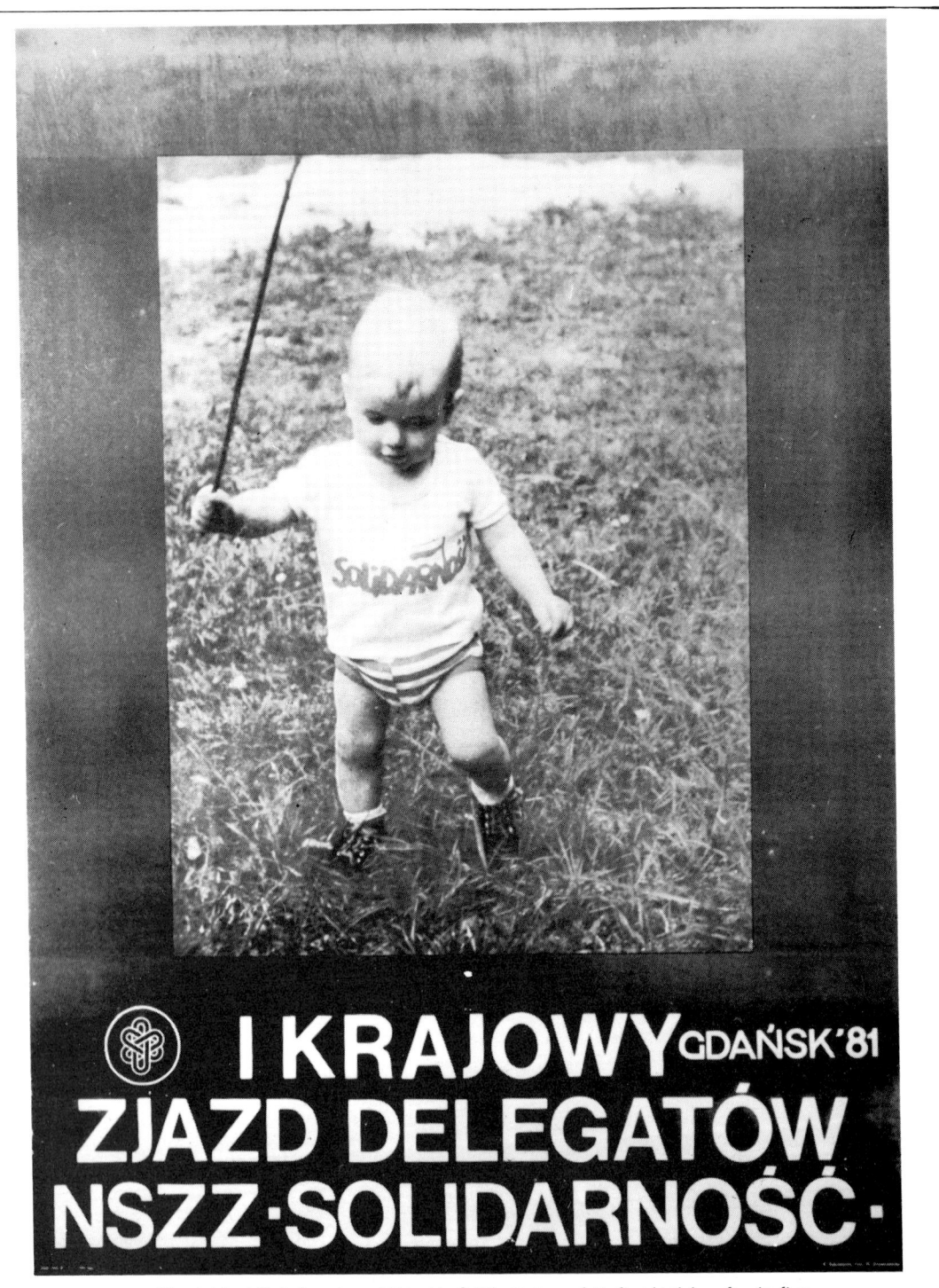

The original "baby" poster published by Solidarity to mark its first birthday after its first annual conference in Gdansk. It was produced in October 1981 and copies appeared all over the country. The government parody — RIGHT — mysteriously went up shortly afterwards.

worry, that he himself was on his way to Gdansk, and that we could catch the next train together. When it arrived, however, I was a bit worried to find the majority of the passengers were soldiers but we boarded it, there were no more problems, and in an hour or so we pulled into Gdansk. I was also concerned that there might be a reception party waiting for me at the station – but there was no one, and having explained to my new friend that I had nowhere to stay we set off for the polytechnic's hostel where he could offer me a camp bed on the floor of his room. But first we had to get there.

By now it was past eleven in the evening as we set off to walk to the bus station, deviating slightly to see the famous ship-yard memorial, an unanticipated surprise for a dark night, and I was beginning to think at last I could relax when we were approached by an aggressive drunk in the process of vomiting over his own clothes. Having considered the best strategy for dealing with this new problem, he con-

veniently collapsed on the pavement, and we found the bus we wanted.

We travelled for about twenty minutes, then alighted, and walked up the hill to the hostel. On the way we passed a building in the process of construction and my friend commented, with professional concern, that most modern architecture in Poland was a disgrace and limited in its life expectancy.

Normally there would have been a night receptionist on duty at the hostel but, fortunately, he or she was nowhere to be seen and we walked straight in. Technically, I should have registered and left my papers at the desk but I was not overly keen to do this. The rooms in the Gdansk Polytechnic hostel were far less luxurious than those at The Riviera but the students were just as friendly. When word got

The posters are fake state copies of Solidarity posters showing a child in an outline map of Poland. They carry the ominously added warning in the top left-hand corner "Don't Play With Fire" and have been prepared by, and surreptitiously posted up by, agents provocateurs in the pay of the government.

around that there was an Englishman in the building the room soon filled with inquisitive visitors and, although I was very tired, I felt obliged to stay up till early morning answering all the questions that were thrown at me.

For the next couple of days I went round Gdansk. I visited the Solidarity building and saw the giant slogans painted on the pavements nearby. One read ''Polish TV Lies'' but the *milicja* were afraid to remove them because of the strength and popularity of the trade union there. I heard more talk of a general strike but if this happened I wanted to be in Warsaw and document it

LEFT — Exhibition of graphics, the Polish national art-form, which (left) commemorates the Gdansk strike of 1970 and the birth there of Solidarity in 1980; (centre) shows a tank inside the international "No Entry" sign; and (right) the anniversary of Poland's 1791 constitution. RIGHT — A woman feeds Black-headed Gulls on the pier of the Baltic resort of Sopot. This lies half-an-hour by rail from the city of Gdansk. BELOW — "DTV KLAMIE" — "Polish TV Lies", a pavement slogan near the Solidarity headquarters in Gdansk. DTV is the equivalent of the BBC. This slogan is one of many which the authorities were afraid to remove.

photographically on what had become my home ground. I didn't know Gdansk and couldn't do the job properly there, but in Warsaw, through my contacts at Mazowsze, I stood a much better chance. I bought a ticket for the evening train.

My last day in Gdansk was spent sightseeing like a conventional tourist. I climbed to the top of a church's bell-tower in the old part of the city and was rewarded with a magnificent view. Afterwards, there was just time to have lunch in Sopot, a holiday resort about half an hour by rail from the city centre, before we returned at four o'clock to Gdansk to catch my train. I went into the public lavatory at the station, the floor of which was a stinking slippery mess of excrement, and realised how the typhoid had spread into an epidemic.

The journey back to Warsaw was uneventful. Before leaving Gdansk I had phoned the American embassy to let them know what happened to Dan's two sons on the train out from the capital but they'd had no reports of the arrest of any American citizens.

For the second time I returned to the sanctuary of The Riviera and learnt that the strike was almost certain to take place. I phoned John who declared it was inevitable and so, on the morning of the twenty-seventh, I made my way to Solidarity headquarters. The trade union was heading for a direct confrontation with the government from which they could no longer back down even had they wanted to; if the strike were not called officially it would still have taken place.

The foto-reporters, as they called themselves, told me to return the next morning, the twenty-eighth, but the twenty-eighth was also the day on which my visa expired and my plane was due to leave at two-thirty the same afternoon. I was now growing anxious for the strike was scheduled to

Solidarity's "foto-reporter" team at their Warsaw headquarters. On the right is the poster which blames the Russians for the massacre of fifteen thousand Polish officers at Katyn in 1940.

begin at twelve o'clock and end at one and, plane or no plane, I was determined to get some good pictures and fly them out of the country the same day. That afternoon I wrote an article on Solidarity for the Western press and, by a stroke of luck, managed to obtain a line to London. Laboriously, I dictated it to a bewildered telephonist – but it was never published. Part of it is printed below.

"When Poland beat East Germany in the World Cup eliminators a roar of triumph rose above the TV monitors on Warsaw Central Station. Next morning the Party-controlled papers reported Polish fans in East Germany were forbidden to wave their flag. Generally Poles have few reasons to smile and no outlet for their frustration. There is a sense of defeatism and desperation which is sadly creeping across Poland. As the number of unofficial strikes increases, widespread official action by Solidarity membership becomes inevitable and, consequently, the number of joint police and army patrols is stepped up.

"Solidarity states it has called for a one-hour general strike for two reasons. Firstly, because the government refuses to take effective action over food shortages and, secondly, because they have rejected the free union proposal for a joint commission on the Polish economy. A token general strike, or even the threat of one, is obviously a way to preserve unity within Solidarity's membership (and its sympathisers) and it also demonstrates to the government the union's continued capability for unified mass action. The token nature of the strike hopefully makes the point without forcing Jaruzelski's "new" government to take drastic action. There is one other important aspect – it shows the Polish people that Solidarity is doing something.

"As the economic situation deteriorates, and as the Russians apply more pressure by restricting fuel supplies (the block I'm living in has had no hot water for a week, and the average wait for petrol is now seven hours), Poles are losing hope, in life, in the future, and to some extent in Solidarity. Yet despite some disappointment Solidarity is seen as the only credible source of information – its news sheets are quickly sold out and its wall posters are read all over Poland.

"Many basic foods are artificially cheap, when they are available, and so when the opportunity arises people buy as much as they can. Not unexpectedly, the crisis is making everyone increasingly selfish, and that selfishness could destroy the rebirth of freedom in Poland.

"Poles are resigned to their fate. They know the Russians would rather not cross the border and be caught actively attacking the Polish working class – it's far easier for them to switch off the fuel supplies. But Moscow may reckon it has no option if Solidarity cannot preserve discipline. The paradox here is that the union will only be able to achieve this if the food and fuel shortages do not grow any worse. There is a delicate balance which allows Moscow to "punish" Poland by restricting its basic commodities but, equally, to bring chaos to the country would defeat the Soviet objective – and after Afghanistan the Russians are doubtless even more wary of direct military intervention.

"If the Russians came then the Poles would fight. The occupation of the country by the Nazis is still an important subject on the curriculum of all Polish schools. The people of Poland have proved once already in the last thirty years that they can rise from mass destruction. As one middle-aged woman told me: 'I worry for the young. But I'm not scared. I was in Auschwitz.'"

The rest of that last night in Poland was spent saying goodbye to friends and laboriously packing my luggage which now consisted mainly of all the books, posters and badges I had been gathering. Seen as a collection, as it was at that point, I realised it was highly sensitive material and I began to worry about the customs officials at the airport who would most certainly confis-

The two sides of Poland in the autumn of 1981. A wet evening in the drab concrete ugliness by modern Marszalkowska Street and a young army conscript takes his girlfriend out for the night. On the right is The Metropole Hotel and to the left of it stands The Forum. On the left are the deserted soft-drink stalls typical of Warsaw. There were always several on Warsaw Station and when no soft drinks were available people often took empty bottles to these stands to have them filled; usually, carbonated water was poured out first and coloured sweetener added afterwards. INSET BELOW — Inside one of the markets in Warsaw. These are state-regulated for the private sale of flowers, fruit and vegetables.

OBYWATELSKI
KOMITET
BUDOWY
POMNIKA
OFIAR
ZBRODNI
KATYŃSKIEJ
PRZY
REGIONIE
MAZOWSZE.

KATYŃ

cate the lot. The poster of Katyn, for instance, which had been given to me by Solidarity in Warsaw, was just too dangerous to carry in my luggage and I arranged there and then to send it to England by another route. Katyn, incidentally, was the place where fifteen thousand Polish officers died in 1940 after Poland was divided under the terms of the Nazi-Russian pact; although the Russians attributed their deaths to the Nazis, recent evidence has shown that the Soviets were responsible. The poster, printed in blood red, was probably the most directly anti-Russian produced by Solidarity; its caption read: "We forgive those who have come to understand". Before I finally went to sleep I checked over all my camera equipment.

LEFT – The blood-red Katyn poster produced by Solidarity which blames the Russians for the massacre of fifteen thousand Polish officers during the Second World War.
BELOW – Solidarity's Warsaw printing press in action on the morning of the general strike, 28 October 1981. The right-hand poster "Poznan 1956" recalls one of the great strikes of the past, the first publicised confrontation with the government.

I went to the Solidarity building first thing in the morning and found the printing press on the ground floor churning out pamphlets which gave the reasons for, and instructions about, the forthcoming strike. They'd been working all night long. Upstairs, the graphic artists were silk screening "telegrams", one of which is reproduced here.
28.10   12-13

GENERAL PROTEST STRIKE. HUNGER STOP. REPRESSION STOP. WE DEMAND THE CREATION OF A SOCIAL COUNCIL FOR THE NATIONAL ECONOMY. OUR PROGRAM: SELF GOVERNING REPUBLIC. THE WHOLE OF POLAND WARNS (YOU) STOP.

I knew that everyone else at that moment was at a conference discussing the organisation of the strike so I waited for a while and when they returned explained I was booked on a two-thirty flight out of Poland. They gave me more publications to

take home and a copy of the letter which is reproduced here.

"SOLIDARITY — Region Mazowsze, Warsaw. Warsaw 28-10-81. To the Polish Community in GREAT BRITAIN/USA.

"The whole of Poland is now waging a war of freedom. The independent self governed trade union "Solidarity" urgently needs help from Poles abroad. We need especially not financial help, but equipment that we can use in our work. Particularly urgently required is photographic equipment. We've discussed our needs with Michael Yardley and we ask you to help him. We must have this equipment as soon as possible, as from day to day the situation in our country gets worse. The following equipment is vital: Canon F-1 with standard lens 55mm f1.2, 85mm lens, 135mm lens, 200mm lens, 500mm f2.8 low light lens; Olympus XA (*they'd seen my tiny Olympus camera and been impressed with it; such a small and versatile camera could be very useful to them.*) 300 metres of Kodak Tri-X; 300 metres of Ilford HP5; Braun 2000 electronic flash.

"Thanking you in advance for your help."

At about ten-thirty that morning I walked back to The Riviera to finalise with Stephan my plans for getting to the airport. We agreed to meet at exactly one-thirty and I gave him everything, except my cameras, to put into his car. This consisted of my overnight bag and four carrier bags stuffed with books. These had all been thoughtfully packed so that most of the superficial contents were "acceptable" books about the war or Polish culture. The other material was not hidden but I had diminished its visual impact by scattering it in less obvious places. However, I was particularly worried about my film. By now I had

BELOW — The telegram produced by the graphic arts department of Solidarity's Warsaw headquarters for the general strike of 28 October 1981. RIGHT — Copy of the letter given by Solidarity in Warsaw to Michael Yardley and addressed to the Polish communities in Great Britain and the United States. It asks particularly for camera equipment and film.

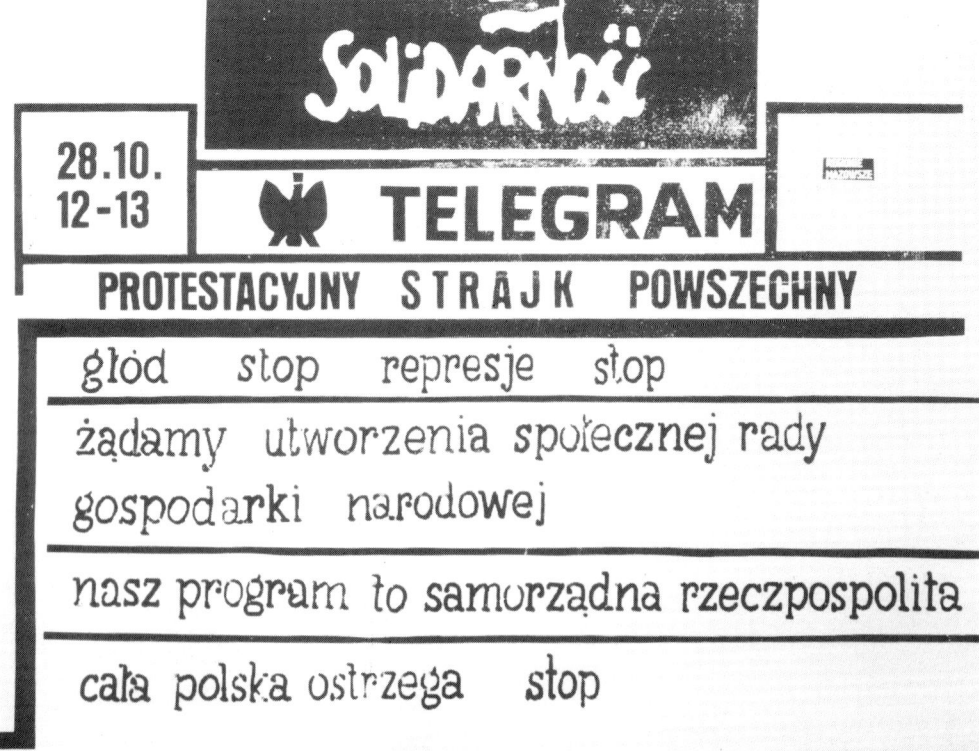

Warszawa, dnia 28.X.1981

Do Polonii w Wielkiej Brytanii

Region MAZOWSZE
Warszawa
ul. Mokotowska 20

Sekcja Fotoreporterska
NSZZ Solidarność
Region Mazowsze
Warszawa, ul. Mokotowska 20

Cała Polska prowadzi obecnie walkę o wolność. Niezależny Samorządny Związek Zawodowy "Solidarność"" bardzo potrzebuje pomocy od Polaków zagranicą. Zależy nam szczególnie nie na pomocy finansowej lecz na sprzęcie, który mógłby służyć naszej działalności. Szczególnie potrzebny jest nam sprzęt fotograficzny. O tych potrzebach rozmawialiśmy w p.Michaelem Yardleyem i prosimy, by pomoc dla nas przekazać właśnie Jemu.

Bardzo nam zależy na otrzymaniu sprzętu możliwie szybko, gdyż sytuacja w naszym kraju jest z dnia na dzień coraz poważniejsza. Szczególnie zależy nam na następującym sprzęcie:

Aparaty CANON F-1 z obiektywem standard f=55 mm 1:1,2 i silnikiem napędowym

Obiektywy f=85 mm, f=135 mm, f=200 mm, f= 500 mm - 1:2,8 albo o więlszym otworze względnym

Pierścienie pośrednie dla makrofotografii

Aparat Olympus XA

Filmy Kodak TRI-X-PAN 300 m

Filmy Ilford NP-5 300 m

Lampy błyskowe Braun 2000

Bardzo dziękujemy z gory za ewentualną pomoc.

KIEROWNIK
Sekcji Fotoreporterskiej
Katarzyna Zenn-Pasternak

approximately forty rolls of it, all black and white and most of it processed, but rather than cut it up in the usual way into short manageable strips I had rolled them up one after another like a spool of 35mm cine-film. This, I hoped, would take up far less space, but I then found myself with a fat circle of film whose diameter was about six inches and far too large. So I split this into two smaller rolls and carefully wrapped each in a silk handkerchief; now they would fit neatly into the side pockets of my jacket. The badges I distributed amongst spare corners of my camera bag, various pockets, and any other conveniently obscure places I could think of — though nothing was actually hidden.

It was half past eleven by the time I had finished and I set off back to Mazowsze. I was just walking up the steps of the building when a voice shouted from a taxi: "Hey, Angolu!" It was one of Solidarity's photographers who bundled me into the cab and we were off before I was really

quite sure what was happening. By a synthesis of his very broken English and my almost non-existent Polish he made it clear that I was to get ready. He, himself, was loading roll film into a large East German Pentacon camera and he paused for a moment to pass me a red-and-white Solidarity armband with the word "foto-reporter" overprinted. This was an honour. He explained that the taxi would act as a kind of mobile base while we dashed round as many factories as possible taking pictures of strike activity.

At our first stop, the Fiat-Polski plant in the Praga district of Warsaw, we both got out and I waited while he ran inside one of

Warsaw. The day of the general strike, 28 October 1981. RIGHT — A lathe operator makes his token protest by sitting quietly beside his machine for an hour at an electronics factory. BOTTOM RIGHT — The gates of the Praga (Warsaw) Central Telephone Exchange. The Solidarity photographer (wearing sweater) is showing his credentials and attempting to gain admittance. BELOW — Solidarity stewards at the Fiat-Polski factory refusing admission to an official Polish television crew who carried on filming outside the gates nonetheless.

the office buildings. He reappeared a few minutes later with a friend and together we went to the main entrance of the plant where Solidarity stewards were refusing access to an official Polish television crew and, subsequently, to various international television representatives. They let us through and inside we met the senior shop steward who was surrounded by about a dozen workers acting as guards. An argument developed about whether or not they would allow anyone in to take pictures and my friend produced a letter from Solidarity's Mazowsze headquarters. They therefore agreed to let just one person through - and I was naturally the one who had to wait outside. I whiled away the time by taking pictures of the TV crews, one of which is printed here, and chatting to a camera team from France, until my erstwhile colleague reappeared and we set off once more.

This time our destination was the Fabryka Aparatury Rentgenowskiej, an electronics factory about a mile away, but when we

arrived the security guard refused to let us in. He was the typical petty bureaucrat in uniform that one finds everywhere. The letter from Solidarity was produced again and, fortunately, several shop stewards appeared to support us. Together we went inside and upstairs in the lift to see the director of the factory. I just kept quiet. The guard knocked on a door and when it opened I saw we had interrupted a management meeting. The director was politeness personified when he read the letter; many managers, especially those with embarrassing skeletons in their business cupboards, had become increasingly afraid of Solidarity for no one at that time could safely predict the outcome of the crisis. It was possible that the trade union would ultimately take up a permanent place in the governing of the country and therefore no intelligent

Jacek Kuron, a leading Solidarity advisor (far left, bald) about to address strikers at the Central Telephone Exchange in Warsaw on the day of the general strike, 28 October 1981. His speech had a tremendous effect on the assembly.

manager could afford to make enemies with it in advance; in addition, some of them were already Solidarity members.

We were at once given the freedom of the factory, to the apparent disappointment of the security guard, and dashed upstairs to the main production line which had come to a halt. My friend reached into his pocket and produced a large alarm clock — it was about half past twelve. The men were busy chatting amongst themselves and completely ignored both us and their work. My friend took several pictures of them all — with the clock in the foreground to make the point. We then hurried back down the stairs and I stopped for a moment to photograph a lathe operator.

We were beginning to run out of time and still had our most important call to make, the central telephone exchange. The taxi screeched to a halt outside the building and the first thing I spotted was a strike notice and several Polish flags. There were no problems here with security men (the

photograph shows my friend having his credentials inspected at the gate) as they were all members of Solidarity, and we went straight in and passed through an enormous room where sophisticated telecommunications equipment was normally being assembled. It was odd to see this huge factory floor at a standstill and I took several pictures until a foreman objected and I was forced to stop.

We carried on walking and after passing the factory came upon a crowd of many hundreds of people listening to two speakers, one of whom was Jacek Kuron, a senior advisor to Solidarity and a founder of KOR, the Komitet Obrony Robotnikow. Kuron is one of the most respected men in Poland and his speech was having a tremendous effect on the assembly but at that moment a horn sounded to indicate it was one o'clock and the strike officially over, and everyone

The author Michael Yardley (second left) poses with three of Solidarity's "foto-reporters" beside the Katyn poster at their Warsaw headquarters.

started to sing a Polish anthem about freedom. The atmosphere was very emotional but I could only partially understand the feelings of the people there. This was my last day in Poland and I was extremely conscious of the opportunity I had been given to witness the making of history and to take a series of pictures which might otherwise never have been seen.

We got back to the taxi in a jubilant mood and returned to the Solidarity building. For the last time I climbed the staircase to Sekcja Fotoreporterska and said goodbye to everyone. I was given yet more material to take with me to England and left promising to return probably in February, or earlier if I could raise the money for the photographic equipment.

Stephan was waiting at The Riviera and we set off immediately for the airport, stopping only once, briefly, at The Victoria. That left me with just one problem — customs. It's an offence to take any Polish currency out of the country so I gave Stephan the six thousand zloty I had left and asked him to keep it for me until I returned. I also asked him to take care of my baby Olympus as I didn't want anyone to find three cameras on me if I was searched. Besides, it seemed an appropriate way of saying thank you; Stephan had been a great friend.

I approached the long table where all the bags are checked before loading. There were only two customs men on duty and as one looked much more officious than the other, I edged slowly towards the better prospect and then stood waiting for ten minutes while the woman to my right had her luggage taken to bits by the man I was trying to avoid. The other man came up to me.

"Have you anything to declare? Any Polish currency?" — "No, just this painting. Here's the receipt and export licence."

One needs an export licence to take practically any work of art out of Poland and I had bought the painting on purpose because I hoped the red tape might prove conveniently distracting. I also knew all my papers were in order.

"Anything else?" — "No." — "O.K."

The next hurdle was passport control. Theoretically I should have registered with the police throughout my stay but I hadn't after Stephan pointed out it wasn't necessary and would only draw attention to myself. If I'd stayed at an Orbis hotel all the time this registration would have been done automatically and it was partly for this reason that I'd earlier justified the expense of one night at the Holiday Inn, anticipating, incorrectly, that they would stamp my visa and hence prevent any awkward questions later.

This time I picked the wrong queue. Inside the box at the barrier sat a senior official with four stars on his epaulet who spent a long time flicking through my passport. Finally, he said: "We have no record of your stay in Poland."

Trying not to appear visibly ruffled I replied: "Oh, that's odd. I've been in the Holiday Inn in Cracow. Here's the receipt." He glanced at it, and for one long moment I wondered which way his decision would go, but he seemed to be satisfied for he then stamped my papers and returned them to me with my passport.

Now there was only the security check which I had not foreseen as a problem. A soldier tapped me on the shoulder and said: "We'd like to search you." Of all the things I hoped wouldn't happen this was the worst. I didn't know what to do with the film that was in my jacket pockets. If they found it I'd have everything confiscated. Very quickly, I slipped the two packets into my camera bag and handed it, along with my carrier bags, to the woman at the X-ray machine. In Iron Curtain countries they use hard X-rays in their security scanners so it was fortunate that the film was already processed. I had no time to get rid of anything else. First they frisked me and then asked me to empty my pockets. I produced a lot of junk and several Solidarity badges, which they picked over but otherwise ignored, and delved down into other pockets. Again they checked through the contents — and indicated I could go. The woman at the machine passed me back my cameras and the other bags and I realised the search had only been for metallic objects.

Later, I discovered the very fast black-and-white film which had not been processed — that is, the four rolls I'd taken that morning and which were in my camera bag — had all been partially fogged.

I walked into the departure lounge, still feeling somewhat anxious and rather tense. Stephan had told me the only place in the country where one could buy genuine Polish vodka was the duty-free shop here where, of course, he had a "friend". I joined a long queue for the last time in Poland and came away with a bottle of "rectified spirit" which I was looking forward to trying out on unsuspecting friends. At last the flight was called and while walking to the airport bus I was surprised to see the rather large English-woman I'd first met on the train to Gdansk — seeing her reminded me how lucky I'd been.

I'd left so soon after the general strike that the Communist bureaucracy had had no time to alert the airport police that the first flight out of the country afterwards would inevitably carry news of the embarrassment to Jaruzelski's government. I heard later that the next day all travellers on international flights were thoroughly searched until one pilot got so fed up with waiting that he went and protested to the airport police who, having stripped half his passengers down to the bare skin, released the remainder with no checks at all.

In all I had spent less than a month in Poland. I'd travelled across the country from Zakopania to Gdansk. I'd seen the queues for food and even waited in some of them. In Warsaw, I had the privilege to work with Solidarity and to make some very good friends at The Riviera, but now I could return to my own country with the material I'd gathered. I had witnessed Poland's suffering and was going back to the comforts of home. Thirty-five million Poles don't have that advantage.

BELOW — Groups of young army conscripts were frequently seen on the streets of Warsaw in October 1981. In this picture, taken on Marszalkowska Street, one of them has just spotted the camera.

six weeks later
CONFRONTATION

RIGHT — The widespread fear of October 1981 was realised six weeks later when General Wojciech Jaruzelski declared a state of martial law and closed Poland's borders to the western world. This photograph, taken from a third-floor window in the "foreign section" of Solidarity's Warsaw headquarters, looks down on Mokotowska Street where a crowd has come face to face with a police riot squad. Photograph by Gamma.

The Author

MICHAEL YARDLEY was born in Copenhagen in 1955. He received his early education in England, in Switzerland and the United States, and eventually returned to England where he attended Westminster School for a year and, later, Goldsmiths' College, London University, where he obtained a degree in psychology. Having tried unsuccessfully to make a living as a freelance writer and photographer, he joined the army, was commissioned into a cavalry regiment, and was posted to a small garrison at Wolfenbuttel near the East German border. While there, he developed his skills as writer and photographer and in May 1981 resigned his commission. He now combines a career as a photojournalist with research into East European politics at the London School of Economics. Recently, he has made several radio broadcasts concerning Poland and his work has also been seen in the *New Statesman, New Society, The Sunday Times*, and on BBC television. His exhibitions have been on show at The Orangery in Holland Park, London, and at the Photographers' Gallery, also in London. When he is not working, Michael relaxes by restoring antique microscopes, pistol shooting, or going to the theatre. He lives in London but continues to travel; his next book will be about the Middle East.

FRONT COVER — Military parade beside the Tomb of the Unknown Soldier in Warsaw's Victory square; October 1981.
BACK COVER — Official Solidarity poster produced to commemorate the union's first birthday.